Sowing and Growing a Garden

New Illustrated Library of Home Improvement Volume 13

Sowing and Growing a Garden

Prentice-Hall/Reston Editorial Staff

Prentice-Hall of Canada, Ltd. / Reston Publishing Company
Scarborough, Ontario

Contributors/H. Fred Dale, Richard Demske, George R.
Drake, Byron W. Maguire, L. Donald Meyers, Gershon
Wheeler

Design/Peter Maher & Associates

Printed and bound in Canada.

The publishers wish to thank the following
for providing photographs for this volume:
American Association of Nurserymen
Better Lawn and Turf Institute
Canadian Association of Nurserymen
Canadian Department of Agriculture
H. Fred Dale
Ferry Morse Seed Co.
Malak
National Garden Bureau
The Netherlands Flower-bulb Institute
Sheridan Nurseries
Yoder Brothers

Contents

Preface

This volume is intended to assist the reader not only to use correct planting and sowing techniques in growing a garden, but also to achieve variety by growing different types of gardens. The planting seasons and viability of the plants discussed here are generally those of the central North American region, with specific variations noted (e.g. Pacific coast, prairies). You should check with your local nurseryman and agricultural experimental station for further details on specific plants and their growing seasons if you live in a subtropical, subarctic or desert climate.

For suggestions on how to plan the best use of the soil and available space for lawn and garden, see Volume 8 of this series.

Planting Techniques

Getting plants to grow well in your garden depends on a number of things. Buying first quality nursery stock and using a good planting mixture (as discussed in Volume 8) are important. But proper handling and planting techniques are just as essential.

Improper handling and planting can kill or maim even the best nursery stock set in the finest soil. The way you start a plant in your garden will largely determine how it will do from then on.

Transplanting well begins as soon as you take possession of the stock. Obviously all plants are living things. They are adapted to their environment — the soil — where their roots thrive on the balance of air and water between the soil particles. They are not adapted to air alone, and can tolerate mixtures used to package them for only a short time. So the first rule of transplanting is to get them back into the soil as soon as possible.

Their roots should be kept covered and moist at all times except for the actual moment of planting for a few seconds until you fill soil around them again. If the plants are delivered to you before you can plant them, store them in a way that will do least damage to the roots.

One such method is called "heeling-in". This consists in digging a shallow trench on an angle in the ground. One end should be deep enough to take the root system, the other end shallow enough to expose the top or trunk to air and light. Fill soil over the roots and water rather a lot to settle it down among the roots. If you can find a spot in permanent shade to do this, so much the better, but make sure there is at least shade from noon on so the hot afternoon sun doesn't dry the plant's tissues.

Another method is to plant temporarily in a container — flowerpot, pail, bushel basket or whatever is suitable — that you can store in a cool, shady area.

Short-term storage overnight between the time the plant arrives and when you plant it can be done in laundry tubs filled with water, or even in a bucket outdoors. If you have a number of plants to set out that you have to carry from planting spot to planting spot, make a slurry of soil and water in a container. Swish the plant roots through the slurry so all the fine hair roots have a coating. Add water as necessary so the coated roots do not dry, and carry them along in the bucket.

Of course, plants delivered with only loose packing materials are the most vulnerable to air damage. But even those in tightly tied packages can dry out, so don't assume that you can keep them a long time in a garage or shed. If it is not possible either to plant them immediately, or to heel them in, open the package at the top and test the packing material for dampness, adding water to it as necessary — it should be distinctly damp, but never soaking wet or bone dry.

If the plant arrived in a plastic package with no packing materials, check to see that there are no punctures or loose ties. If there are, the chances of the plant living are poor indeed and you should return it to the nursery at once.

Also check balled and burlapped and container plants for dryness. The soil ball inside the burlap or in the container should also be damp, and there should be no signs of dried needles on evergreens. Nor should there be long shoots with pale foliage on any nursery stock — this indicates it has been stored at too warm a temperature and that new growth has been forced indoors, wasting the plant's vigor.

1-1. When to Plant

While it is theoretically possible to move any plant at any time of the year if you can move a large enough volume of earth so the roots are not disturbed or exposed to the air, in practice there are two basic planting seasons. The first and best for most plants and most climate areas is in early spring as soon as the ground can be worked and before there is any sign of new growth. The second is in late summer or in fall when woody plants approach dormancy. The latter time is slightly different for evergreens which begin a dormant period at the end of August for about a month or six weeks, after which they produce new root growth until freeze-up. Deciduous trees and shrubs don't become dormant until later. This time is signaled by the change in leaf color, or by a killing frost, whichever comes first.

While fall planting is very successful in milder climate areas, it is not so safe in colder ones because there is less time after leaf fall until freeze-up. And it is during that period that woody plants establish new roots in their new location, essential to their survival over winter.

There is also a group of unrelated trees and shrubs that do better with spring planting in any climate area. These include both fruiting and ornamental cherries, birch, poplar, magnolia and rhododendron. It has also been our experience that garden roses do far better with early spring than with fall planting.

Nursery stock that is grown in containers theoretically can be planted even in midsummer, although again it has been our experience that keeping generally to a spring or fall planting schedule works best. However, in a pinch, where you discover, say, in late spring that a plant hasn't survived, it's nice to be able to go out, buy a container plant and set it in place so there is no hole in the planting over the season.

Special attention must be paid to watering, as such plants have a restricted root run and may wilt badly on hot, windy summer days. Wrapping the trunks with kraft paper, and spraying the foliage with water from the hose will help them over their critical first summer. The ground around the roots should not dry out, but it shouldn't be kept sopping wet either. Keep to the wet-dry cycle suggested in the previous volume.

Maintain the irrigation right until freeze-up for all woody plants set out that season, for plant roots continue to grow as long as the soil at their level remains above freezing. It is especially important for evergreen plants to go into the winter turgid — that is, with their tissues as full of moisture as possible. When the ground is frozen, their roots can take up no more, and what they lose from evaporation due to the winter sun and wind must come from the tissues of the plant. If there is too little, they suffer what is usually called "windburn". In severe cases it can be fatal, although usually it is only disfiguring.

1-2. Where to Plant

While some evergreens and a few deciduous plants can survive in wet or waterlogged locations, most garden subjects need a dryer soil that has more air spaces in it. So be sure to plant only bog plants in bogs. Among evergreens, eastern white cedar, balsam, bald cypress, hemlock are suitable, and

These snapdragons were bred for outdoor endurance and greenhouse quality.

among deciduous trees and shrubs you could try swamp red maple, white birch, willow, some poplars and dogwood shrubs.

For other plants in extremely heavy clay and low areas where air has trouble entering the soil, it may be necessary to install drainage tiles under the soil. Certainly surface drainage should be good. In these sites it is not enough simply to excavate a large planting hole; this only acts as a kind of catch basin.

Even if surface drainage is good, break up the soil at the bottom and sides of the planting hole, mixing in some sand and peat moss. This will help make the transition from planting soil mixture to the garden soil and allow

penetration of the roots, rather than having them confined to the pocket of good soil you planted them in.

But unless your garden soil is first quality topsoil, it will pay you to make up a planting mixture. One of the best is composed of equal parts loam, sphagnum peat moss and gritty or sharp sand. These materials may be mixed on any level surface using a spade, and should be in a damp condition before being used.

It is also important to choose a planting spot that is free of heavy shade and root competition. Some plants can tolerate a certain amount of shade and even some root competition, but most cannot.

And the kind of competition offered by

These Annabelle shrub hydrangeas are also known as "snowball" hydrangeas.

competing plants is quite different, too. Shallow-rooted trees, and particularly vigorous ones such as poplars and soft maples, dominate their areas. Even wispy grass has a hard time competing. Deep-rooted oaks, on the other hand, whose lower branches have been removed to let in light, may permit a great number of shade-tolerant plants to exist beneath them (see Chapter 8 on shade gardening).

Cold-tender plants should be placed on the north or east side of buildings where they will get shade from the winter sun and wind. So should fruit trees that flower early such as peaches and cherries that are grown beyond their hardiness area.

There is no point in trying to grow plants that are at home in alkaline (sweet) soils in acid-soil areas unless you can amend the acid with limestone. And anyone trying to

The same basic principles hold true for vegetable gardening as for flower gardening: plants need sunlight, moisture and the proper nutrients.

grow acid-soil plants in alkaline areas is doomed to failure unless the native soil is removed and replaced with an acid peat soil.

1-3. Start with a Big Hole

There's an old gardening story that says it's better to put a 25-cent plant in a $5 hole than a $5 plant in a 25-cent hole (which perhaps should be updated for inflation). It illustrates our point: the planting hole should be at least twice as big around and twice as deep as necessary to accommodate all the plant roots without crowding, folding them over or cutting them off. If your inclination is to lift a flap of soil and stuff the plant's roots in, restrain it.

Bear in mind that the roots not only take up all the water and minerals that enable the plant to live and grow, they also anchor it against the wind. And if the roots are crossed, they may actually strangle the plant. Small roots circling a large one eventually act as a tourniquet and cut off the flow of liquids.

To plant a bare-root tree, shrub, evergreen or rose, back fill the excavation with planting mixture, packing it so there are no large air spaces. Build a cone of planting mixture in the hole large enough and firm enough to support the plant at the proper height.

This can be determined on trees, shrubs and evergreens by a stain mark on the trunk that indicates the height at which these plants stood at the nursery. They should sit at the same height in your garden (with the exceptions noted below) or just slightly lower. Planting too deeply effectively changes the grade on the plant, and roots developed to have so much earth over them may suffocate with more. In other words, don't bury the plant.

1-4. Exceptions to the Rule

Unfortunately one rule doesn't apply to all plants and the only way to remember which is which is to memorize or to consult a list. Roses are the chief exception. In all cold climates where the ground is frozen solid and air temperatures go down to zero or below, rose canes die. If they die back below the bud union – the bump on the stem where the desirable variety shoots originate from – the rose is dead and gone for all garden purposes.

So roses must be planted deeply in cold areas. In fact, the roots should be set low enough so the bud union itself is below grade, one, two or three inches depending on how severe the climate is. Deep planting not only aids winter survival but encourages the top desirable variety to put out its own roots. If it does and these are vigorous, the rose is much better equipped to stand severe weather, and any new shoots from these roots will still bear the desirable flowers.

When planting a sapling, fill the hole to lower root level with soil mixed one-fourth to one-half with mulch or peat moss. Work planting mixture around roots and tamp firmly.

Another exception that should be planted deeply is a grafted young tree peony. This is a woody cousin to the herbaceous peony. It is hard to grow from seed and slow if grafted on seedling roots. But top grafts make fast growth when grafted on herbaceous peony roots. Deep planting encourages the tree peony top to grow its own roots. Virtually the same situation applies to lilacs that are grafted on other roots.

Dwarf fruit trees are the reverse kind of exception. They are manufactured plants, too. But they must stay on the dwarfing rootstalks all their lives in order to remain dwarf. Planted too deeply, they will develop roots from the trunk. These will be the same kind of roots that an apple tree would have and you could wind up with a 40-foot tree when you thought you were going to have one only 8, 10 or 12 feet high.

When the hole is three-quarters filled with the planting mixture, water in thoroughly to eliminate air pockets.

1-5. Plant the Stake Too

All saplings (or bigger trees), evergreen trees and broad-leafed shrubs that might be up-rooted by winds in a storm should be staked. The time to drive the stake is while you are placing the plant in the hole and while you can see the roots so you don't drive the stake through them later.

The stake should be long enough to support the entire trunk of the plant and still allow for driving it several feet into the ground below the excavation for firmness. It should be sturdy enough to support the plant in a wind without too much give. Obviously it shouldn't be brittle enough to snap off.

Set the plant on the cone so the roots spread naturally out and down. Preserve as many hair roots as possible; these are the feeding roots. Woody roots may be pruned as necessary. This should be done to trim ragged ones and to remove any that are broken, or that girdle others. Woody rose roots may be pruned quite hard to encourage lots of new growth.

Make sure the best-looking side of the tree, shrub or evergreen faces the way you want it to. Spreading evergreens should have their longest dimension across the wall of a house.

Then shovel planting mixture into the hole around the plant – it helps if you have a helper who can hold the plant in place at the right height.

When all the hair roots and most of the woody roots are covered, soak the material in the hole. You can do this with water, but it is better for the plant if you use a transplanting solution very high in phosphorus which helps cut transplanting shock and encourages new root growth. Make this up by dissolving a soluble fertilizer powder such as grades 10:52:17 or 10:45:15 at the rate of a tablespoon per gallon of water.

When the soaking sinks away, tamp the wet planting mixture, then fill the hole almost to the brim. Again soak with transplanter solution and tamp, while holding the plant firmly at the correct height. Repeat as necessary until the planting mixture is level with the surrounding soil. Do not use dry fertilizer in the planting mixture.

At this point it is an advantage to mold the soil under the plant into a shallow, saucer-like depression. This helps catch rain and irrigation water so that the plant is easier to water.

If you are planting a number of seedling trees that won't get careful attention, make a depression by scooping out some soil individually or in a trench so that all the weeds and grasses are removed just above the plants' roots. This cuts down on competition for water during the first summer, and also helps trap rain water. You can take this a step further by splitting a piece of old asphalt shingle, tearing a hole out of the center and fitting this around the stem of the plant. It will keep weeds suppressed for many years, and if it is

arranged so the center is depressed, it will funnel rainwater into the root area.

Or you could use some sort of mulch around the new plant to discourage weeds and retard evaporation. Examples are round stones, chunky peat moss, wood or bark chips, strawy manure, or partly worked compost.

Arrange the ties to the stake which should be on the windward side – in most locations, the west side of the plant. Ties should be firm but flexible so they do not cut into the bark or rub it away. They should also allow for an increase in the trunk size.

You can make good ties by threading sturdy wire through a piece of old garden hose. Other possibilities are an old bicycle inner tube or plastic skipping rope. A good way to tie the plant is with an S-shaped loop around the stake, crossed, then around the plant and tied, or vice versa.

If the plant is a tall tree and one stake is not enough to hold it firm against a heavy rain or snowstorm, guy wires should be substituted. They should be fastened to a flexible tie around the tree at one or more points along the trunk, and then anchored to sturdy stakes driven into solid ground. Tie bits of cloth or bright plastic to the wires so everyone can see they are there.

Many deciduous trees and evergreens will need to be staked for the first two or three years only. Dwarf fruit trees should be staked all their lives. Extremely fast-growing saplings, such as poplars and hybrid honeylocusts, should be staked for five to ten years.

Outside of watering as climate and soil conditions indicate, and checking ties spring and fall to make sure they are secure, the plant should need no more attention. It will not need any more fertilization than that provided by the transplanter solution for the first year.

If it came from a reliable nursery, it should need no pruning either. But you may, if you wish, remove lower branches totalling up to one-third of the twig wood on deciduous trees and shrubs. On trees brought back from the wild this is a necessity so the leaf-bearing area is reduced in proportion to the loss of roots suffered when you dug the trees up.

Hedge plants can be sheared back one third to encourage heavy foliage.

1-6. Planting B & B and Container Plants

The basic procedure is the same in planting nursery stock, whether it comes balled and burlapped or in containers, except that you don't need the cone in the bottom of the planting hole.

When the B and B plant is properly placed and the hole almost filled with planting mixture, undo the knot of burlap around the stem and fold it back down so it will be covered with soil.

Container plants need different treatment depending on whether they come in metal cans or in fiber pots. Those in cans first have to be removed, and this requires what seems to be rough treatment. Turn them over (or on their sides if they are large). Rap the edges of the can all around the bottom with a trowel with sharp blows; then rap the center. It should be easy, now, to pull the roots intact from the can by grasping the stem at the soil line with one hand, and pulling hard while holding the can firm with the other hand. Sometimes the roots come out so easily they startle you; other times they require several hard tugs.

Upend the plant and set it on the backfilled, prepared planting mixture in the hole and proceed as for bare-root plants.

Those in fiber containers may be set into the ground, container and all. But it makes it easier for the roots to penetrate the sides and bottom of the container if you slash them in many places with a sharp instrument. Set the container in place in the hole, allowing for the rim of the pot. This should not show above the

These marigolds have been packaged in a convenient strip of 12 peat pots. The pots are broken off and planted pot and all.

soil surface after planting or it will act as a wick and dry the soil around the roots. If this method is inconvenient, you could simply cut or break the rim off and proceed as before.

It sometimes happens that when you try to remove a so-called container-grown plant from its pot, the roots and soil separate. This indicates that the nursery or sales station stuffed the plant into some soil inside a pot and that it wasn't grown in a container at all. You have two choices: simply plant it as though it were a bare-root plant in the first place (this is okay if the plant is healthy, the bark plump and the cambium juicy and green), or you can return it and demand your money back. (To test the cambium, lift a flap of bark with a thumbnail.)

Occasionally garden plants are sold in plastic or red clay pots. The latter can be treated like metal cans, or simply broken away from the roots by a really sharp crack. Plastic needs more effort but can be shattered, too.

1-7. Planting Hedges

Plants used to grow hedges are not different from other plants in the garden; they are merely ones that tolerate growing close together and being clipped regularly. Their value to you will depend on their ability to keep growing heavy foliage at the same time you are constantly removing wood and leaves that plant energy has gone into making.

Thus you can see it's important that the soil be prepared thoroughly before you plant them. It is possible to grow a hedge with plants set in individual small planting holes, depending on future fertilization and watering to keep them vigorous.

But it is much better for the plants, and easier to set them out in the pattern you want — straight line, curve, zig-zag, etc. — if you lay a string line out on the ground or between stakes, and then excavate a trench to accommodate their roots.

Again, the planting area should be much wider and deeper than is strictly necessary for the root spread. Here's an ideal planting method to strive for: excavate the trench two feet wide and two to 2-1/2 feet deep. Break up the soil on the bottom so that there is drainage. Place a two- to six-inch layer of strawy manure in the bottom of the trench. Next place a six-inch layer of topsoil (of the peat moss-sand-loam mixture). Now fit the plants in, adding more planting mixture as needed to raise them so the stain line on the stems is in line with the soil surface.

How close you set them will depend on their size. Very small plants can be set six inches apart. Set two-foot to three-foot plants a foot to 18 inches apart. Set tall plants two to 2-1/2 feet apart. Soak with the transplanter solution, top up with soil, soak and tamp and top up again.

Make the first pruning immediately after planting, topping the plants and reducing their volume by about one-third. Aim for a profile shape that is a rough cone, the narrowest part at the top and rounded off.

The rounded tip will help shed snow and heavy rain. The narrower top will let light and air into the lower branches and thus help them to keep good leaf production.

As suggested, hedges need watering and annual fertilization in spring or late fall just as other garden shrubs do. Since they are competing so close to each other you might give them fertilizer both spring and fall. A lawn type will do fine, sprinkled on the ground surface between and on both sides of the plants.

An annual pruning will keep most hedge plants looking neat (see the previous volume for Chinese elms). This should be done before new growth appears in spring, which is also the time for any heavy, remedial pruning. In late June or early July prune lightly to remove any long, unwanted growth. Repeat this in September if necessary. Dead foliage or branches may be removed at any time, as may storm-damaged stems.

Eastern white cedar, a popular evergreen hedge plant, tends to retract its foliage in fall in preparation for winter. If the browning foliage that is being shed bothers you, you can cut it out. It will, however, separate from the live foliage on its own, and fall to the ground where it builds up a natural mulch.

In cool climates hedges do not usually need mulches other than the natural foliage drop.

But any of the materials mentioned earlier may be used if you wish.

A hedge of quality plants, well planted and cared for, is good for half a century at least, so the effort that goes into the planting is well worthwhile.

Sowing Seed, Planting Flowers, Laying Sod

2-1. Raise Your Own

The easiest and cheapest way to get plants growing in your garden, whether grass, flowers or vegetables, is by sowing seed that is freely available from nursery sales stations, local stores and mail-order houses. And it is one of the most satisfying parts of gardening to raise your own plants, perhaps a few more than you need, so that you can give some to friends and neighbors.

The simplest way there is to get flowering plants in your garden in summer is to sow the seed outdoors where you want the plants to bloom. Prepare the seedbed ahead of time so that all is ready for planting time.

Since annual flowers (and those other plants we treat as annuals) are shallow-rooted, no deep preparations are necessary, although they certainly won't hurt. But if your soil has reasonable drainage, thoroughly cultivating the top six to eight inches is sufficient.

Most annuals do not need a particularly rich soil, but they do need good drainage and moisture holding soil (see Chapter 3 in Volume 8). So mix into your garden soil some form of humus-making material such as sphagnum peat moss, peat loam, rotted compost or other material. If the basic soil is heavy, also use some sand. Till with a rotary cultivator or hand dig and rake out lumps and stones. It is not necessary to have the annual flower bed absolutely level nor perfectly smooth. Little ridges of soil help hold the earth and seeds against a heavy rainfall.

At this point you have to decide whether you want to raise a large number of plants in the seedbed to act as a nursery for the rest of your garden so you can transplant extras later, or whether you just want the number of plants required for the seedbed area.

Plant the seeds as thickly or thinly as indicated. Look at the package information and directions. Tall plants need more space between them than short ones, as is obvious, but so do plants that spread. Sweet alyssum, for example, only grows a few inches high, but it may spread until it is a foot across by September.

Don't bury the seed. Many failures are due to covering the seed with two inches of soil or more. A good rule is to have no more soil over it than twice the thickness of the seeds themselves. With a very fine seed, this means a bare dusting of soil.

Large seeds such as marigolds and zinnias are easy to plant individually. But smaller ones, such as petunias, flowering tobacco and portulaca are quite fine, and unless you buy pelleted seeds (the pelleting is a coating that in effect makes the seed larger and thus easy to handle individually), you'll have to devise a method of dribbling it out. Try picking up a pinch between thumb and

Even narrow spots can become gardens. Here, petunias and sweet alyssum beautify space between fence and walk.

forefinger. By rubbing the two fingers across the pinch as you move your hand down the row, the seed is dispersed. When the seedlings appear, remove enough so the remainder are spaced to give them room to grow.

Broadcasting annual flower seed is never satisfactory, although it is sometimes recommended for ''an old-fashioned garden''. It is better to make a formal place: a shallow trench can be made by drawing a trowel lightly across the area to be planted. This doesn't have to be a straight line, if you want the plants in a circle, oval, angle or wavy pattern. But remember that just as plants need space between each other in the row, so do they need space between the rows.

If the bed is to be seen from one side only, tall plants should go at the back with progressively shorter ones at each end and at the front. If the bed is to be seen from both sides,

the tall plants should be in the middle and the rest graded down to both sides and both ends.

After seeds are planted and you have lightly covered them, tamp the planted area so the seed and earth are in intimate contact. Then soak the area with a very fine nozzle sprinkler, so that there are no washouts. Unless rain is regular and sufficient, it is a good idea to dampen the seedbed every day or two until the new plants are well up. In warm weather, fast ones like zinnias and marigolds will appear in a week. Slower ones, such as snapdragons, petunias and portulaca, may take up to three weeks, so don't give up too soon.

Keep the seedbed weeded. If you are afraid you won't recognize the flowers and pull them out as weeds, confine the weeding to between the rows, being sure the rows are marked off with stakes at each end.

With few exceptions annual flower seeds may be planted on or just after the latest frost date for your area. In areas where that occurs early in the spring, plant annuals between May 1 and June 1 when the ground will be warmed up and the weather more settled. Most summer annuals need warm ground and air to do their best.

2-2. Planting Vegetable Seed

While preparation of the seedbed is much the same for vegetables as for annual flowers, they need a much richer soil, and, for root crops, deeper preparation. Growing vegetables in a small plot is what is sometimes called "intensive cultivation". It uses up soluble minerals and humus materials over the season and these must be replaced annually.

Strawy barnyard manure was the standard fertilizer and soil improver in days gone by. It is still very good if available free or at low cost. Fresh material should be mixed with garden soil in fall; it is safe to use rotted manure in spring before planting.

But for most city gardeners manure is far too high-priced to make any kind of economic sense, especially if you are raising vegetables to help out on the high cost of food. The cheapest and one of the best soil improvers is home compost which costs nothing but the labor to make it. Otherwise use an alternate form of humus-producing material (see Chapter 3 in previous volume on gardening) plus a chemical fertilizer when preparing the soil. Use one with high middle and last figures (examples are 5:10:15, 4:12:10, etc.) at a rate determined by dividing the first figure into 100. Using the first example, you divide 5 into 100; the answer, 20, means you spread 20 pounds of fertilizer on every 1,000 square feet of garden. Then incorporate it, along with the humus, into the garden soil.

In general, vegetable seeds may be planted earlier and deeper than flower seeds. Many are able to grow in colder soil and can withstand light frosts. Round-seeded peas, onions, lettuce, carrots, beets and radishes are quite hardy and it's worth taking a chance on losing them to plant some a while before the typical May 24 planting date. In addition, corn plants, once started, can withstand frost and potatoes planted in the ground but not yet sprouted above it are safe from freezes.

Tender, hot-weather plants such as curcurbits — cucumbers, melons, squash — tomatoes, eggplant and peppers should never be set out until well past the latest-known killing frost in your area; in fact not until the ground and air have warmed up. But these are long-season plants and so you will not likely get a harvest from them by starting them from seed outdoors. Either buy them as started plants or start seeds yourself indoors early — see below.

It is even more important to have vegetable seeds spaced well than flower seeds. To be tender, tasty and of good size, vegetables must have room to develop, sufficient root space and no competition for light. This is why weeding is so important, especially if you can't irrigate. The best vegetables are harvested from plants that grow quickly and without setback from seed to maturity.

As with flower seeds, vegetables should not be buried. However, deeper planting is normal. Radishes need only be covered; carrots and lettuce just dusted with soil. But peas, beans and corn should be set one to two inches deep in a trench. Plants can be as close as six inches to a foot in a tiny garden, but 1-1/2 to two feet is better. Rows in small gardens need only be far enough apart to let you walk between; in larger gardens allow room for a tiller to go through to cultivate and keep weeds down.

2-3. Corn, Beans, Potatoes, Tomatoes

Corn can be planted in rows, especially if you are growing a lot of it. Make the rows into a block as nearly square as possible, as corn is wind-pollinated.

It takes two men to lift this gigantic pumpkin.

In small gardens it is more convenient to plant a group of four corn seeds roughly in a circle, six to 18 inches apart depending on the size of the corn plants and the size of the garden. It is possible to plant only one hill and still get good pollination this way. But you can plant as many hills as you have room for. Corn should be set on the north or east side of a garden, so smaller growing vegetables will still get lots of sun.

Treat beans like peas, except that they should be planted much later in the season, late May to mid-June. Beans are not only sensitive to frost, but may rot in the ground before germinating if it is cold and wet. In a small garden, alternate one seed of green beans with one of yellow. If you are short of space you could plant the beans between the rows of peas. The peas will be finishing as the beans come on.

Potatoes are cool-weather plants and can be started early. If you are planting a large number and using the same place for them each year, use certified "seed" potato slices. Otherwise, healthy tubers showing sprouts from the bag in the kitchen will provide seed stock. Use them either whole or in chunks or slices that contain a growing point or eye. They should be set four to six inches deep and have earth (or a mulch) heaped up around them after they are well up so new tubers are well covered — they turn green and are considered poisonous when exposed to light.

Radishes are a short-season crop; they mature in about three weeks, so you can sow them repeatedly except in midsummer when they tend to become hollow and hot.

Tomatoes, probably everyone's favorite, are easy to grow from healthy seedlings. Like all vegetables they do best in full sun all day, but you can get fruit from a minimum of six hours' sunlight daily. There are many varieties, some ripen fruit in as short as 50 days from setting out plants. Suit the varieties to your climate area. In long-season areas you can set out some early, mid-season and late varieties to extend the harvest.

Tomatoes can be grown tied to stakes or let sprawl. In general, you get more fruit on sprawling plants; you get bigger fruit and quicker ripening on staked plants. The latter are usually cleaner and freer of damage from slugs. Keep staked plants to one stem by removing the sucker shoot that grows between the main stem and the leaf branch. Catalogues describe tomatoes as determinate or indeterminate. This means they either reach a certain height and stop of their own accord, or they keep on growing at the tip shoot as long as the season holds up. The latter need either a lot of space or a tall stake.

Tomatoes need an even supply of moisture in the ground to grow good fruit free of blemishes. Irrigate when summer rains fail.

2-4. Planting Grass Seed

Planting grass seed is no more mysterious than planting any other seed. It's just that there is so much more of it.

The idea is to scatter an appropriate amount evenly over the prepared seedbed, so that, allowing for failures and what the birds eat, enough seedling plants will survive to spread out and cover the ground. In most mixtures that contain only bluegrasses and fescues, three to five pounds is sufficient for 1,000 square feet of lawn. If you are planting only fine-seeded bluegrass, three will be enough, if creeping red fescue or its newer varieties, you'll need five pounds. If you are making a temporary lawn of coarse-seeded perennial ryegrass, use 10 lbs.

The easiest way to get even coverage is to use a seeder-fertilizer cart set for the proper poundage. But there is no reason why you can't seed by hand.

Put the seed in a shallow container such as a basin and walk the seedbed area, picking up handfuls and scattering it lightly as you go. If you have no idea how fast to toss it out, mark off a 10-foot by 10-foot area (100 square feet). Take one tenth the seed for the 1,000 square feet, and try making it cover the 100 square feet evenly so you get the feel of how much to cast.

Some gardeners like to insure even coverage. There are at least two ways. You could mix the seed with an equal volume of soft sand, loam, peat loam or processed sewage, and seed the whole area twice, once walking to and fro, and the other back and forth. Or you could simply divide the seed in half, covering the whole area twice, as above.

A light rolling or tamping with a board or a stick will help place the seed in very close contact with the soil. Little ridges left when raking will act as water catchers and prevent the seed washing off in light rains or irrigations.

A fog or very fine mist nozzle is best for the hose. The seedbed should be slightly damp before seeding. Then fog or mist it until water stands briefly on the surface of the ground. Repeat each time the surface dries. This is the only time in the life of the lawn that it should get shallow watering, but you don't want the seed to dry out once it has started to sprout.

Repeat this until there is enough topgrowth of grass to cut with the mower set at two inches. Then switch your watering to that of the alternate wet-dry cycle — apply enough water to soak the ground six inches deep (usually one inch) and don't repeat until the grass is about to wilt. On the average this means watering once every week or 10 days if rains fail. Clays may need the water less frequently; sands more.

Grass seed varies in the time it takes to sprout, from a few days for perennial ryegrass in warm, moist weather, to two weeks or more for bluegrass when the ground is cold. This is one of the reasons perennial ryegrass is included in packaged mixtures — it shows up quickly and makes the gardener happy quickly. Its disadvantage is that it crowds the slower, better grasses, and takes nourishment and water from them.

The best time of the year to start a new lawn is in late summer, around Labor Day, when conditions favor root growth and quick sprouting. The second-best time is in early spring as soon as you can work the ground. Grass seed is very cold hardy, and ordinarily freezing temperatures won't hurt it.

Weeds will very likely appear among the new grass even though you weeded the seedbed or used weedkiller on it. Sometimes home gardeners blame the seed they used, feeling the weed seeds must have come with the grass. But the facts are that weed seeds are constantly blowing around from weedy yards, vacant spots, areas around billboards, even cracks in pavement. And they also come from your own soil: every time you cultivate you turn up buried weed seeds that are still alive and sprout when brought to the surface. Hand-cut them as they appear, or wait until after your new grass has been cut several times to apply a selective weedkiller.

If you are trying to grow grass seed where there is no irrigation available, or on slopes where it may wash out, a mulch may help. Chopped straw, wood chips or similar materials can help conserve moisture if applied after a rain. For banks and small areas, you can cover the seeded area with burlap, or similar material, and peg it in place. It can be dampened down with a minimum of moisture. Grass will grow right through it.

Most good, perennial grasses take up to two years to mature, so if your newly-seeded lawn seems to be rather thin, give it time and good maintenance. Where crab grass is a problem, a combination of cutting the lawn high (crab grass seedlings die in shade) and using a pre-emergent crab grass herbicide in mid-spring will keep it under control.

You can thicken up an old lawn or introduce a better strain of grass into it by seeding, too. But simply scattering seed on top of the existing grass blades is mostly a waste of time and money. Either turn the sod on thin areas upside down, exposing loose soil, or drag a saw-toothed (scarifying) rake over the areas to be seeded, opening up the soil. Seed as for a new lawn, except that you'll need only about one pound per 1,000 square feet.

In renovating an old lawn, first cut it. Then apply fertilizer and water it in. Weedkiller comes two or three days later. Wait a week or 10 days and then overseed.

2-5. Starting Your Own Seed Indoors

To make the most of a short summer, most gardeners prefer to get a head start. Rather than plant annual flower seeds where they are to bloom, they start them indoors on window sills, or they buy started plants grown by greenhousemen. These are available at various sales stations in mid spring, very near to or actually in bloom.

The secrets of growing your own plants so they are vigorous and sturdy at planting-out time are the time you start them and the conditions in which you grow them. Most dwellings are too hot and too dry.

Good places to grow seedlings are in a cool but sunny window sill where cool air can be admitted on warm days, and in a cool basement room under fluorescent lights. High temperature should be under 65° with a drop of five to 10° at night. Humidity should not be below 40 per cent although you can get by on 30 to 35. At higher temperatures and lower humidities, plants have poor leaves and lanky, soft stems.

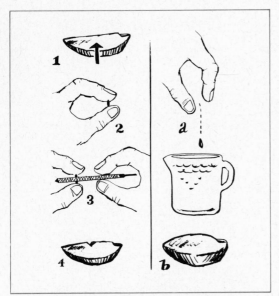

To aid hard seeds in getting started, they may be nicked with a file or softened in water.

Don't start the seeds indoors too soon. Six weeks before planting-out time is just about right unless you have a greenhouse and/or greenhouse growing conditions. The poorer your indoor growing conditions, the later the starting time. Take into account the number of days the seed takes to germinate, and add it on to the starting date – that is, start earlier.

Some gardeners like to start seed fairly thickly in a shallow, round pot. When seedlings have developed four leaves, they are separated by pulling apart, and then planted in individual containers, or grouped, several to a container.

Larger plants such as tomatoes, pepper and eggplant, which must have a start indoors if they are to bear fruit before frost, may be planted one or two seeds to an individual pot. The second seed is for insurance; if both germinate, transplant or nip off the extra.

2-6. Setting Out Started Plants

Whether you buy them or grow them, seedling plants are handled the same way. Bearing in mind height and spacing discussed earlier, prepare the planting holes in the flower or vegetable garden with a hand trowel. As with woody plants, they should sit at about the same level they did before, or slightly lower, except for lanky tomatoes which may be planted deeply enough to effectively shorten the stem.

Make sure the soil in the containers is moist so it will stick together. Cut between each plant growing in a flat or fiber box, and pry up one at a time. Holding it so the soil and roots are kept intact, set it in the hole. Gather a little garden soil over and around the root system and stem, pressing it enough to hold the plant firmly upright. Water with the transplanting solution described in Chapter 1, a half cup to a small plant, a cup to a large one. Tomatoes, peppers, climax marigolds and other tall plants that need support should have the stakes set at planting time.

Plants in clay pots can be loosened by rapping the bottom with a trowel. Those in plastic may need a knife passed around the edges to free the roots. If the plant really sticks and you're afraid you'll damage it, split the pot and peel it off the roots. Firm new soil around and over the roots by tamping, and leave a slight depression around the plant to help in watering.

Water carefully for a week or two, keeping the soil moist at least until new roots are established. Then water only when rains fail.

2-7. Laying Your Own Sod

As discussed in the previous volume, starting a lawn from seed or from sod requires exactly the same preparation right up to the moment of planting. When the seedbed is level and smooth and damp, and has been allowed to settle for a couple of weeks, you can ask for delivery of the sod. Don't make the mistake of ordering it before your preparations are complete; you may find it sitting in the driveway growing into itself or rotting in the rain that keeps you from preparing the bed.

This plug of Highland Colonial bent grass is mowed to a half inch, too short for most grasses.

Laying sod is not as critical as applying tile to a wall. You can piece where you need to, and the pieces will knit together. However, it's better to use a string line, at least for the first few rolls.

Peg the end flap to hold it in place. Unroll the sod against the string line, adjusting the peg as necessary. Repeat with the second roll, omitting the pegs unless you're on a hill. Make the butt joint tight but not so tight the sod bunches up. Tamp lightly with a board nailed to a piece of 2″ × 4″ as you go along. Sod across rather than up and down a hill, pegging with wooden stakes as necessary.

Water each complete section until the ground is quite soggy and keep traffic off. Water frequently after the sodding is completed.

Some people like to dust topsoil where the pieces of sod join, even using grass seed there. But it is not necessary if the joints are tamped level. The sod will soon take root in your soil and send up new growth that will quickly fill small gaps.

You can tell when it has knitted – a slight tug will fail to move it. At this point reduce the watering to normal lawn watering but keep traffic off for another couple of weeks. Cut whenever the blades grow above two inches, except when the ground is soggy and the mower wheels might sink in or lift up edges. Sod is fertilized and sprayed with weedkiller in the sod nursery so should not need treatment on your grounds for some time.

2-8. Transplanting Grass for Repairs

Just as you can repair thin or dead patches in an established lawn with grass seed, so you can with sod. Small pieces can be cut from a roll of sod and used as plugs in thin or dead areas by making room for them with a hand trowel.

But for larger areas, it is better to remove the old sod using a Dutch hoe or square-mouth spade. Then cultivate the earth underneath so it is loose and pulverized. Water before and after piecing the sod.

It is possible to grow your own sod in small quantities to have it on hand for repairs. Simply follow the directions for planting seed at the beginning of this chapter, but on a very much reduced scale. Use only bluegrass or red fescue or a mixture of the two. The sod is mature enough to use the second year after sowing the seed.

Another source for sod on a small scale is volunteer grass plants you take from the flower or vegetable garden (if it is in fact lawn grass and not crab grass, twitch grass or a coarse meadow grass), and pieces of sod removed when you edge around trees, hedges, flowers, etc.

3 Planting Bulbs

There is a group of tender bulbs, or bulbous-like plants that add to our summer flower garden. These include tuberous begonias, caladiums, gladiolus, dahlias and canna lilies.

Because they are frost-tender, they must either be abandoned each fall or carefully dug, cleaned and stored away for the winter. The method of restarting them into growth the next season depends partly on their characteristics and partly on their size and the room you have indoors.

Gladiolus, for example, perhaps the most commonly planted tender summer bulb, needs no indoor start (except for gardening in the very far north). Kept close to freezing in a completely dark room, their sprouts should be minimal until outdoor planting time. Their "bulbs" are properly called "corms"; they should be checked periodically over the winter and any that ooze resin, or that become woody or corky and light in weight should be discarded. If they were dusted with chlordane before storage in fall they should be free of thrips (sucking insects that ruin flowers and weaken corms to the point of destruction) in spring at planting time.

Less frost-tender than the others, glads can be planted out quite early, even though the ground hasn't warmed thoroughly. One way to speed their flowering is to set the corms about six inches apart in a three-inch deep trench. Barely cover them with a porous material such as sand or vermiculite. This lets the sun in to warm the earth. As sprouts grow add a little more covering in stages until the ground is level.

As the season advances, plant the corms deeper — up to four inches — and cover the trench. Wires between stakes at each end and each side of the row will help keep the flower spikes straight and protect them from wind damage.

Gladiolus does best in a sandy loam soil that has adequate summer moisture but will get along on most soils. It should be prepared as for a vegetable garden with a general fertilizer or bulb food or 5:10:15 worked in ahead of time.

Because glads are so attractive to thrips, a systemic insecticide spray should be used on them from the time the new green shoots appear until killing frost.

After frost, pull or dig the plants. Cut off the tops, leaving a four- to six-inch handle. Let the corms with roots attached remain in the sun or an airy, sheltered area to dry for a week to 10 days. Then twist off the tops and the old corm with roots and discard. Save the plump, high-crowned new corms. The little "bulbs" attached to the roots are called "cormels". The largest may be saved to grow in a trench like peas the next year. They will eventually form corms — they may produce flowers the next year or the year after.

Dust corms with insecticide and store cold but above freezing, alone on wire shelves or in dry peat moss or sawdust.

Glads don't change color despite the experience of many gardeners which suggests this. In fact, some colors multiply faster than others, and some varieties tend to die out.

3-1. Tuberous Begonias

Rivalling glads for popularity among tender summer bulbs, tuberous begonias are even more versatile. They can easily be grown in pots on balconies, on verandahs, in window sills, in hanging baskets to trail down, on stakes as specimen plants in the garden, or massed together under the high shade of a tree to brighten a dull location.

While glads produce one flower spike (with up to 20 or more florets) and then are done, begonias, once started, will go on flowering until killing frost.

While it is possible to start their tubers directly in the soil outside, after all danger of frost is over, this delays their blooming. And in fact shoots may be too lanky to be manageable by that time.

At planting-out time, buy started tubers in pots. Or start your own indoors six to eight weeks ahead of time. Do this by placing a number of tubers in a flat tray of peatlite (see Chapter 4) or coarse potting soil mixture. Nestle the tubers, round side down, concave side up, rocking them to make a cradle in the soil so almost all the tuber but the top is touching the soil, which should be kept damp but not soaking wet.

Place the tray in bright light and 60° to 65° temperatures such as under fluorescent lights left on 16 hours a day, or in a north or east window sill. When several leaves appear and the tubers indicate they are rooted by resisting a strong tug, separate them and transplant, with soil attached, to separate pots of peatlite or coarse soil. Pots should be shallow but wide — about four inches in mouth diameter. This time set the tubers so there is about 1/4-inch of soil over the top of the tuber, and tie them to bamboo canes set in

the pots. Begonias have shallow but widespread roots, and their stems are succulent and brittle, so handle them with care.

At this transplanting begin using a diluted fertilizer solution once every two weeks in place of normal watering. You could alternate with a grade 20:20:20 and a 10:52:17. Some people like to use a fish emulsion fertilizer instead of the 20:20:20. Give plants in window sills a quarter turn daily to keep them growing straight.

When all danger of frost is over and the ground is warm, set begonias outdoors. To put them in the ground, knock them out of their pots and set them, stake and all, just slightly lower than before. Good locations are in high shade from a tree, in part shade or in sun till noon, such as on the north or east side of a building.

If the plants are to remain in pots all summer, transplant them to a larger pot — one with a mouth diameter of about six inches. A shallow bulb or azalea pan is fine.

Begonias often have more than one shoot from the tuber. If the tuber is large you can allow two stems, especially if you want a stockier plant with lots of flowers. You can also cut the tuber in half with a new or sterilized razor blade, dust the cut end with sulphur and then plant the two pieces. Or, to obtain the largest flowers possible, pinch off the extra shoots, keeping only the largest. Also pinch off the smaller single female flowers (with the triangular ovary behind) so all the plant strength goes to the larger, showier male flowers.

Keep begonias growing as late in the season as you can, for they make most tuber growth in fall. This may mean protecting them against early frost or bringing them in and growing them under lights until November. It also means dusting or spraying with a fungicide to protect them against mildew.

When you want to make them dormant, withhold water so the soil in their pots dries out. Then, when the stem and leaves dry, take out the tubers, clean all traces of the old stem from the tuber to prevent rot. Brush off the dried earth and store the tubers singly in dry peat moss at about 40°. Higher storage temperatures, often recommended, encour-

Large garden tulips that bloom in May and June should be planted in October. (Photo by Malak)

age new sprouts to show too soon. Also, it is advisable to dust your tubers with powdered sulphur to help reduce a tendency to rot.

Tuberous begonias can be grown from seed to flowering in one season by starting the seed, as fine as pepper, in shallow containers indoors in January or February. Tubers may also be sprouted early and shoots cut to root in sand and peat moss.

3-2. Dahlias Are Fast

Dahlias are big, showy flowers that grow from tubers you save over winter or buy in spring. Like tuberous begonias, they may also be grown from seed started early indoors (around March 15) or from cuttings rooted from shoots taken from the tubers started into growth on a window sill or under fluorescent lights.

You can start tubers growing indoors to get a head start on summer if you have the room. Dahlias are vigorous growers and big plants, so most gardeners wait until around the end of May when they can plant outdoors.

Since they are big and vigorous they need a well-prepared plot, preferably with manure dug in the fall before. Or use compost and chemical fertilizer such as bulb food or tomato-potato fertilizer.

Each tuber must have a neck — a piece of the old stem — attached for it to grow. Make the actual planting hole about six inches deep and place the tuber flat in the hole with the neck turned up. Drive the stake at this time just back of the neck so that the shoot will grow up along the stake. Fill with good soil or prepared planting mixture. Tie the shoot periodically as it grows, but loosely enough to allow the stem to grow in diameter.

Maintain a good supply of soil moisture as the plant grows. Use a soluble fertilizer once a month, or broadcast a bulb food over the surface and scratch it in once or twice over the season.

Dahlias do best in full sun and with some wind protection. You can get big flowers by disbudding and keeping the plant to one stem. Disbudding consists of removing all but the end bud of any one flowering shoot. You can do this with your thumbnail when the buds are just big enough to be seen.

Remove faded flowers and keep the plant growing as long as possible to strengthen the tubers to keep over winter. After frost blackens the foliage, dig out the tubers carefully. Cut the tops off so that about six inches of stem remains attached to the cluster of tubers. Any tubers that break off are useless and should be discarded.

Carefully shake or break off excess earth once the clump has dried. Do not try to divide the tubers in fall; instead wait until spring when the new shoots appear — each division must have one or it won't grow.

Dahlias are difficult to keep over winter in heated basements. Try to keep them as cool as possible and examine them for shrivelling periodically over the winter. Sometimes a light sprinkling of water will help plump them up.

There are also dwarf versions that do not need staking that are useful for bedding or to make a dwarf, annual hedge.

Dahlias are subject to powdery mildew in muggy climates and should be sprayed with a fungicide or dusted with sulphur over the season.

3-3. Canna Lilies

Canna lilies are big showy plants that are often the mainstay of public park display beds. Some have colored or spotted foliage and the flowers are huge. Their popularity is waning, although there are some new, dwarf kinds that are more suitable to small gardens.

If anything, cannas like an even richer soil than dahlias, plenty of moisture and a hot location. They don't do well where summers are cool.

They, too, grow from tuberous rootstalks which can be kept over winter indoors. And, like dahlias, they are large and vigorous, qualities which make it difficult to start them indoors early unless you have lots of room or a greenhouse. Started plants can sometimes be found at sales stations. Or you can start last year's tubers where they are to bloom after the ground warms up.

The best cannas we ever grew were planted in topsoil that was six inches deep over rotted barnyard manure. They were watered regularly and had a teaspoonful of chemical fertilizer sprinked over the soil around their roots twice during the growing season.

Given adequate water and fertilizer, cannas can be grown in deep boxes or large pots for patio and balcony gardens. But they do take up a lot of room.

After frost blackens the foliage, dig canna clumps and cut off the tops, leaving six inches to a foot of stalk attached to the roots. They can be stored in boxes, dirt and all. If this isn't feasible, wash most of the earth away with the hose, dry and then store cool. Divide them in spring before potting up or planting outside. Each piece should have one ''eye'' or growth bud – two at the most.

3-4. Less Common Summer Bulbs

Caladiums, valued for their large, highly colored and multicolored leaves, grow from woody tubers, and need roughly the same treatment as tuberous begonias. They do well in even shadier spots, and like begonias, must not dry out. But beware of keeping them damp, especially in clay soils, as the tubers rot easily.

Also like begonias, they need regular fertilization to keep them producing their leaves and to increase bulb size. Tubers may be divided so each section has two or three growth buds, but a large tuber will produce a big display of leaves. They, too, may be brought indoors to finish the season, but their leaves are thin and dry up quickly in dry indoor air. Withdraw water to make them dormant. Caladiums may be stored like begonias.

Amaryllis, properly called ''hippeastrum'', is generally used as a winter-flowering indoor bulb. If sprayed against narcissus bulb fly,

however, it will benefit from a summer outdoors in its pot. Do not plant it directly in the ground where its roots will spread all over the place, making it hard to repot without cutting off roots in the fall. With lots of sun, water and monthly fertilizing, it will probably bloom again outdoors. If the leaves do not brown naturally by fall, withhold water to induce dormancy. Store the bulb dry, in its pot, turned on its side in a cool room for three months. Then bring it to light and warmth, watering carefully to bring it back to growth and bloom in the window sill.

Tigridia, tritonia (or montbretia) and acidanthera are all corms with stalks that bear small, sometimes multicolored flowers, occasionally grown among evergreens, in a mixed summer flower garden and with gladiolus. Treat them as you would glads.

3-5. Planting the Hardy Bulbs

There are two groups of hardy, perennial bulbs: those that bloom in the spring, some before all the snow has gone, and those that bloom in summer and are chiefly lilies. All must be planted in the fall (although lilies are sometimes available for spring planting). In general, the earlier they bloom, the earlier they must be planted. Thus daffodils, hyacinths and the little bulbs should be put into the ground in September; the big, garden tulips that bloom in May and June should be planted in October; lilies should be planted as soon as they are available, which is usually late October. If necessary, holes should be prepared ahead of time and covered for safety, and some soil put away against the frost for covering the bulbs later.

There are two ways to approach planting these bulbs. The first and simplest is to figure on no more than two or three years' good bloom at the most and perhaps only one. Certainly in very shady yards where the bulbs stand no chance of competing with roots of trees and shrubs, you could regard bulbs as winter annuals, planting fresh stock each fall,

Tuberous begonias are popular summer bulbs because they continue flowering until killing frost. (Photo by Malak)

Dahlias grow best in full sunlight and with some wind protection. (Photo by Malak)

and cutting off foliage the next year as soon as bloom is over.

For such temporary use it is only necessary to plant the bulbs as deep as required for frost protection, five or six inches for tulips, hyacinths, lilies and daffodils, and four or five inches for the little bulbs. If the drainage is good, no further preparation is necessary. Nor is fertilization, since the bulbs come with the next year's bloom built-in.

You can use a bulb-planting tool which lifts out a core of soil; you pop in the bulb, flat side down, pointed end up, and replace the plug of soil. Or you could use an ordinary hand trowel. The soil should be damp, not only to make it easier to lift plugs out, but to encourage root growth since it's essential if the bulbs are to survive the winter.

Not all these bulbs are hardy in every locality, although most lilies and tulips are, as far north as gardens can be grown, if they are planted deeply and given a winter mulch after the ground has frozen.

Deep planting not only gives added winter protection, but, along with a thorough preparation of the soil *under* the bulbs, can give up to 10 years of good bloom from the same planting. Note the emphasis on the soil underneath — that is where the bulbs' roots spread and seek moisture and minerals, which along with sunlight enables them to replenish themselves and thus provide flowers the next year.

To do this deep planting, excavate a minimum of 18 inches deep and as large an area as needed to take the bulbs. Lilies should be no closer than a foot apart — 18 inches is not too far and two feet gives them more room to expand. Tulips can be set as close as six inches for an immediate clump effect, as can daffodils, but give them a foot to two feet for longer term effects. Hyacinths multiply slowly, if at all, in northern climates and can be set six to eight inches apart. The little bulbs need four to six inches.

Break up the soil in the bottom of the planting hole and mix in some bulb food or potato-tomato fertilizer, stirring it into the broken material. About a teaspoon per bulb is a fair measure. Water if the soil is dry.

Then back fill enough loam-sphagnum peat moss-sand mixture so it is about six inches deep when slightly compacted. This should leave about 12 inches to the surface. Now nestle the bulbs into the mixture so they are firm. Remember: place the pointed side up, and where tulips are to face forward, put the flat side out so the first, big leaves will face out.

Rather than making a rectangle or a plain circle, try plantings in oval, kidney-shaped and irregular-shaped holes for a more interesting spring show.

Then fill in on top of the bulbs with more soil-peat-sand mixture, watering as you go to settle the soil. Light tamping will help. Overfill the planting area so it is mounded on top to allow for settling, and label the planting so you'll know what you've planted and where.

Next, sprinkle some more bulb food, potato-tomato fertilizer, or wood ashes and superphosphate on top of the planting. By the time it works its way down to the bulb root level, the fertilizer you put under the planting soil will have been used up. (Never allow dry fertilizer to come in contact with the bulbs themselves, or any part of any plant — it has the effect of burning by drawing water out of the plant tissues.)

Deep planting such as this not only makes it possible for the bulbs to renew themselves each year, it offers extra frost protection, discourages them from sprouting tops in a long, warm fall, a winter thaw, or too early in spring when a mild spell will only be followed by a deep freeze.

After flowers fade, remove them high on the stem, but keep all the leaves intact for food-making. Only when they turn brown naturally should you remove them. Then cut them off rather than pull them out — pulling leaves a direct-line hole through the soil right to the bulb and can cause trouble from disease or insects or both.

Lily foliage likely won't brown off before a killing frost as lilies grow well into the fall, even after light frosts. Once they are frost-killed, remove the foliage as for tulips.

Most bulb beds will benefit from a winter mulch, as mentioned above for severe areas. Since snow is an excellent insulator, one of the best mulches can be made from the branches cut from the family (and neighbors') Christmas trees. Interwoven over the bulbs, they help trap the snow and shade it from the sun so it doesn't melt so easily.

Where more protection is needed, heaps of leaves can be anchored over the plantings with chicken wire and stakes. It is usually best to do this after the surface of the ground freezes to keep it from being a winter haven for rodents.

3-6. Naturalizing Bulbs

If you have a large garden where not all the grass gets cut as soon as it grows several inches high, or if you have ground near a stream or river or under a deep-rooted, high-branched tree, you might like to plant some spring-flowering bulbs in a natural-looking, apparently unplanned way.

One of the old methods to achieve this was to take a handful of bulbs, usually daffodils, and roll them out across the ground, planting them where they stopped. When doing this, you may have to adjust their location a good deal so they aren't clustered in one spot and sparse in another. You can make the planting as deep and elaborate or as simple as you want, adding new bulbs each year.

In plantings by a stream, it is just as effective to plant three to a dozen bulbs in a grouping. This makes a splash of color with many flowers in one place that is more effective to the eye from a distance or when driving by, than single bulbs spotted here and there.

3-7. Bulbs for Cutting

If you have space for a separate cutting garden, or even for a row or two in the vegetable garden to plant some extra bulbs, you'll have plenty of flowers for the table without robbing your display flowers.

For a cutting garden you can buy the bargain bags of mixed colors since you're not trying to have them bloom at one time or be all of one color. In fact, for cutting, it's an advantage to mix them.

This is also a place where you can use small bulbs separated from the remains of an old planting, or to plant the bulbs left over from pots bought in flower last winter and spring.

Plant these only as deep as necessary for winter protection. You won't be trying to get them to bloom years hence. And then when you cut them, take as many leaves with the flowers as you wish. As soon as you need the space for vegetables, dig out the remains of the tulips, daffodils, etc., and throw them on the compost pile. Little or no care is required after planting except to be sure there is enough moisture in the soil for root growth right at planting time.

Balcony and Patio Planters

Growing plants in containers has long been popular in Europe and Japan where garden space is in short supply. And while window boxes for plants have periodically appeared here, it is only recently that container growing has caught on.

As individual plants, multiple plantings (of several plants to one container), or groupings of many plants in separate containers, mobile gardens are extremely flexible. They are far easier to look after than a garden in the ground. They can be used to decorate steps, porch, patio, boathouse; they allow you to garden where space is extremely limited, on rocky ground or on an apartment balcony where ordinary in-ground gardening is impossible.

For the summer commuter, they make it possible to have splashes of color among the greens of grass, shrubs and trees, while keeping maintenance to a minimum. In the tiny city lot with a minimum of sunshine, the containers (say, of annual flowers) can be moved to catch the sun and so provide summer color where it would be impossible to grow good annuals in the ground.

You don't even have to raise your own plants to have a good container display. You could, for example, buy florist-grown pots of spring bulbs — daffodils, hyacinths and tulips — to set in the containers in spring. Replace them with summer annual flowers for July and August, and then replace them again with

A small tomato plant that can be grown in a patio will yield two dozen or more fresh tomatoes in a season.

florist-grown chrysanthemums for the remaining time till freeze-up in fall.

Mini-vegetable gardens are possible in containers of varying sizes. A minimum you could aim for would be green onions from sets of multipliers, leaf lettuce, radishes and tomatoes. But the enthusiast with some space

In a small garden, alternate one seed of green beans with one of yellow or purple; beans may be planted between rows of peas since they will start to produce just as the peas are finishing.

This striking patio planter is made from irregularly shaped stone slabs mortared together.

The "tree" geranium is well suited to grow in a container, but must be protected from the wind.

These large, open pots will show off their flowers well in their terrace garden setting.

4-1. Flowers In Containers

Bright, flowering plants are the commonest kind grown in containers. In theory you can grow anything in them that you can grow outdoors in the same conditions. This includes all the common summer annuals starting with the big three, zinnias, petunias and marigolds, and going on from there.

In practice, though, it is better to select the shorter or dwarf kinds if there is a choice, since they are more wind resistant. A three-foot zinnia that is wind-firm in the ground might very well be uprooted from a container unless staked securely, whereas a dwarf or mid-size kind such as Thumbelina or the Buttons series would be all right.

Part of the reason is the smaller rootspread of plants grown in pots. Part is that good potting soils are usually lighter in weight than garden soils. And part is that containers, by their very nature of standing above the ground, raise the effective height of the plants so they catch more wind. The latter effect is multiplied on apartment balconies and other exposed positions.

could try virtually every vegetable that grows in a regular garden with the exception of the space users such as pumpkin and tall corn. Greens can get along on a few hours of sunshine a day. Root, seed and fruit crops require more (full sun is best), but you'll get some kind of harvest with six hours' minimum direct sunshine.

Even a vegetable garden can be grown in containers. The containers should be eight to twelve inches deep.

Mixed plants in the same container should have approximately the same needs as to sun and water.

This tub of cascading blooms can be moved to any spot in a garden or patio that needs brightening.

While mixed plants in the same container should have roughly the same needs as to sun and water, you can vary heights with very good effect. Ageratum, alyssum or portulaca makes an attractive, flowering base from which upright plants such as geranium, snapdragon, larkspur, verbena, stocks or poppy can grow, in a full-sun situation. For a colorful container in shade, try impatiens (dwarf variety) as background for tuberous begonias, coleus or caladiums.

It is not necessary to put everything into the

Try to plant sweet corn in square blocks, as it is pollinated by the wind; plant seeds about six inches apart.

Tall plants in containers (such as these tulips) may be uprooted by wind partly because good potting soil is lighter than garden soil, and partly because they are higher and catch more wind.

For small city gardens that have limited amounts of soil, plants in containers are the answer.

same container unless it is very large or you want to particularly. Plants in individual pots can be arranged and then rearranged easily. Some can be retired to a non-show place once they are past their best, and easily replaced with others that are more attractive.

Even if you do have a large container to fill, it is a lot easier, particularly on a balcony, to place the separate pots inside the large one. By using an attractive covering material such as wood or bark chips, peat moss or stones, you can raise or lower individual pots to account for their smaller or larger size so the rims are all at the same height. Fill the material around and over the pots to get exactly the same effect as you would by planting them all in the same soil in the container. Yet each can be watered separately according to its needs, and they can be rearranged or changed as you wish. They can also be brought indoors at the end of the season, if necessary.

In the same way a small garden can be created on a balcony, patio, flat rock or pavement where no plant could normally grow by assembling a number of individual pots so they please your eye. With even a rough container knocked together with pieces of lumber, and the filler materials mentioned above, the plants will appear to be growing together in a common soil. Such a garden can even be stepped, so that the end, quite high, takes advantage of a blank wall. But remember that if light comes only from one direction, as in window sills indoors, plants must be given a one-quarter turn daily so that they grow upright with straight stems rather than bent to the light.

While most summer annuals do best in full sun, there are some that bloom well in part shade. And since most apartment balconies are not open to the top, and get sun from one side only, these will perform better. The list includes anchusa, wax begonia, coreopsis,

While most summer annuals do best in full sun, some bloom well in part shade. Among them are wax begonia, petunia (shown above) and pansy.

calendula, clarkia, cosmos, pinks, dusty miller, larkspur, lobelia, petunia, pansy, phlox, salvia, snapdragon, sweet alyssum and verbena. In heavy shade try balsam, forget-me-not, lobelia, flowering tobacco, impatiens, pansy, and coleus and caladium for their leaf colors.

4-2. House Plants Outdoors

House plants can benefit from a summer outdoors; in their own pots or set inside other containers they can be arranged with each other or with annuals and other summer plants you discard in fall. Or they can be interplanted in a mixed grouping in a large container to please your eye.

Garden perennial plants are not so adaptable, nor are roses unless you are prepared to regard them as expendable. It is certainly possible to grow roses in containers and get flowers the first summer from newly purchased plants. But unless you have a piece of garden you can use to bury them for the winter, they will not survive winter in a container above ground in any but the very mildest climates.

Shrubs and trees are possibilities if you have the space. They vary as to their ability to survive all year in containers. In general the hardiest will live for a great many years that way and without special protection. Blue spruce and its varieties are the most satisfactory among evergreens. The combination of confined root space and pinching back of new growth each spring will keep them dense and dwarf for many years.

Hybrid American ash is among the hardiest of deciduous trees. But you can experiment with many kinds so long as you are prepared for failure. And sometimes plants do seem capricious.

4-3. Hanging Baskets — Plants at Eye Level

There is a special attraction to plants that are visible at or above eye level, so much so that a

A striking and imaginative use of a tree stump: red geraniums planted in colorful tin cans and hung at various levels.

Hyacinth, daffodils and tulips are combined here to give bright, pleasing splashes of color. (Photo by Malak)

The special attraction of plants that are visible at or above eye level has led to the development of a whole special mode of container gardening.

Even a common kitchen sieve can become a practical and attractive container; this one is filled with petunias.

whole mode of container gardening has been developed for containers either supported from beneath or suspended from above.

These are often planted with a number of different plants, some of which offer trailing tendrils, such as ivy or vinca. But they may be devoted to a single plant, especially a variety of tuberous begonia called "pendula" or "hanging-basket begonia". And a delight it is, trailing rose-shaped flowers from every side at a level where you can examine them without bending to the ground.

If the planting is mixed, it's a good idea to include plants that require the same general cultural directions. Shade-loving ferns won't mix with sun-loving geraniums without one of them suffering. Nor will begonias do well with cactus. But you could, for example, take a hoya (wax plant) from indoors, or a rooted cutting of one, to provide trailing stems around dwarf geraniums and/or cascade petunias for a location in full sun all day.

Pendant begonias and fuchsias like a cool, airy summer location of part shade, or sun till noon only, and you could interplant them or alternate them if you have a number of hanging baskets. Other possibilities for shade include dwarf impatiens, browallia and lobelia with blue flowers, and the accommodating wax begonia or "busy Lizzie" which will grow virtually anywhere. The perennial ground cover known as "periwinkle" *(Vinca minor)* will trail or climb, and rooted sections of it can easily be taken from the ground to plant in containers. Its relative, *Vinca major,* has two-colored (variegated) foliage and pink or blue flowers, and can be used as a trailing plant in either sun or part shade.

4-4. Climbers in Pots

Most perennial climbing plants are not practical for pot culture in cold climates since they do not grow enough in one year. But there are some annual ones that are satisfactory. Perhaps the easiest are morning glory and scarlet runner bean, the latter supplying not only foliage and red flowers but edible fruit.

You can arrange climbing strings on a framework attached to the container so the whole thing is a unit and can be moved as such, or you can simply locate the container near a balcony railing or patio upright support that will accommodate the climber. Sweet peas, canary-bird-vine, cardinal climber, cup-and-saucer vine, kenilworth ivy, moon-flower are all possibilities. And if you want to combine growing food with a climbing vine, grow cucumbers vertically (gourds can also be grown this way).

4-5. What to Grow Them In

Virtually anything that will hold soil and yet has drainage holes in the bottom can be used to grow plants in. We've had equal success with expensive planters and one-gallon, round oil cans (thoroughly cleaned and with holes punched in the bottom). Fiber pots such as nurseries use for commercial plant production will last one season, and they, like the cans, can be painted to suit your décor, or left in their natural brown color.

Other temporary or one-season containers can be found in bushel and half-bushel baskets, and in various plastic products. For example, lettuce and radishes – or a few low annual flowers – can be raised in plastic dishpans with a series of holes drilled in the bottoms with a drill and bit.

The same treatment makes a plastic pail or small size garbage can an excellent container for a large plant, such as a citrus tree, and the handles make it easy to transport. Plastic ice cream containers do the same for small plants.

Red clay pots are traditional and excellent in larger sizes – small ones dry out far too quickly in summer weather (see double-potting below). In large sizes red clay becomes quite heavy. This is an advantage when using lightweight soil mixes as it helps to keep plants from blowing over, but a disadvantage for moving. Red clay is porous and allows moisture to escape so that plants will need watering more frequently (this is a strong advantage when plants are brought indoors for the winter as it helps prevent waterlogged soil). Unless you are very particular and require the pots to be smooth and perfect, buy florist grade if you can find them. Most flaws don't matter, and they make the pots much cheaper.

Plastic plant containers now come in sizes ranging from tiny cactus pots to large patio boxes, and in many effects from the cheapest green or brown brittle plastic to heavy kinds that imitate concrete, plaster and wood. Prices also vary widely from a few cents to $60 or more for heavy plastic self-watering kinds. Most are durable and quite satisfactory.

Wood planters are more traditional again. California redwood octagonals are among the best for chrysanthemums and potted trees. But watch to see the band that holds the pieces of wood together is brass or copper. Steel bands that are finished to look like the other metals rust through in a few years and the whole planter falls apart, even though the wood still hasn't decayed.

Being most resistant to decay, redwood, cypress or cedar lumber are best if you want to make your own boxes and planters. Other woods may be used if you treat them with a preservative inside and paint or stain them outside. The preservative should be applied some time before planting so it has all soaked in before the roots come near it.

Redwood or wicker can be used for hanging baskets; plastic or pottery drawn out like strings of toffee, solid containers of clay or metal, driftwood or hollowed-out logs are possibilities. Plastic mesh baskets are currently popular because they are long-lasting, but they're not as attractive as the old-fashioned wire mesh. The latter will last through three or four seasons, and although they rust, the color matches the moss lining.

For most summer plants, containers should be at least six inches deep, which will accommodate the roots reasonably well, and hold enough soil so it doesn't need watering several times a day. But containers for mixed plantings and for vegetables should be eight to 12 inches deep.

Start hardy trees off in six-inch to eight-inch-deep planters if they are seedlings, moving them every couple of years to a larger size. A two-foot to four-foot evergreen should be in a planter about 18 inches across and the same depth. Deciduous trees will eventually have to go into half-barrels or even full barrels, or the equivalent in masonry. Roses need a minimum of 18 inches depth except for miniatures which are happy in standard pots.

Instead of actually planting in decorative containers, of course, you can merely set the separate pots inside, which cuts down on labor in spring and fall, and in the case of wood, reduces the tendency to rot. Instead of filling window boxes with soil and transplanting into it, you could arrange to place a board across the box at the appropriate depth. Circular holes cut in the board would catch and hold pots by the rim. Metal hangers that will hold pots in place are available to attach to house or garage walls.

4-6. Soils and Soil Mixtures

While it is possible to get away with simply taking a few shovelfuls of earth from the garden to put in the planters, this is seldom satisfactory in the long run. Since the plant roots depend entirely on the small volume of material in the planters, the right combination of materials to supply minerals, water and air is very important. The soil, for example, must hold a great deal of moisture between the particles so it doesn't dry out right after watering, and at the same time it must not remain waterlogged. It must latch on to the soluble minerals from fertilizers so that they are slowly available over a period of time rather than locking them up in an insoluble form or releasing them at once.

One of the best mixtures is exactly the same one we've been talking about for planting in the ground itself: equal parts clay loam, sand and sphagnum peat moss. The peat should be broken up quite finely and damp. In small planters, extra peat moss will help hold moisture better. This mixture will have very little plant food (soluble minerals) available, and plants growing in it should be fertilized on planting and once every two weeks thereafter.

A potting soil containing fertilizer can be made up as follows: two parts loam, two parts peat moss, one part gritty sand, 1/2 part dehydrated cattle or sheep manure and 1/8 part bone meal (for acid-soil plants omit bone meal). All materials should be sifted carefully together, the peat moss being dampened first. Plants growing in such a mixture should not need more fertilizer for at least two months.

Sometimes nurseries sell sterilized, ready-prepared potting soils and these, while more expensive, are more practical for apartment gardeners who have neither loam nor mixing space readily available.

The disadvantages of most standard potting formulas are twofold: they will vary in their fertility depending on the quality of the loam used. And in large containers they are too heavy to move conveniently. A number of lightweight artificial soil mixtures have been developed. The best one for indoors and out, was developed at Cornell University and is called Cornell peatlite. It uses standard garden sphagnum peat moss available in many sizes; vermiculite (medium) available as insulation at building supply stores at under $3 for a large bag; and perlite, a light, white volcanic rock available at horticultural suppliers at about the same price, plus some chemical additives available at horticultural suppliers. Here's a recipe for two gallons of Cornell peatlite, enough for several large pots:

- 1 gallon damp, broken-up peat moss

- 1/2 gallon vermiculite

- 1/2 gallon peatlite

- 2 teaspoons fertilizer grade 10:10:10 (or 3 tspns 7:7:7)

- 1-1/2 teaspoons superphosphate

- 1 tablespoon ground agricultural limestone

- 1/2 teaspoon iron sulphate (ferrous)

- 1/32 teaspoon soluble trace elements (optional).

- Omit the limestone for acid-soil plants.

These pots are held by special metal hangers designed to attach to house walls or garage walls.

All ingredients must be mixed thoroughly. You can do this by pouring them back and forth from one garbage can to another, or by shaking slowly back and forth inside a plastic garbage bag.

Seedlings grown in peatlite need no more fertilizer for two to three months. Larger plants will need fertilizing again after eight weeks. Peatlite is virtually sterile. If you move a plant from regular potting soil to peatlite, wash all the old soil from the roots first.

Peatlite can be used when made, or stored damp in plastic bags.

4-7. Planting In Containers

Planting in containers is done exactly the same way as it is in the ground with the exception that roses and other grafted plants will have only the lower roots covered. In other words, they are planted shallower.

The container size is determined by the size of the plants to be grown, both in depth and in mouth diameter. Don't stuff roots, forcing them all together to make them fit; nor should you put a small plant in a container far larger than necessary to take the roots comfortably. Typically, a small, young geranium plant in a large container may spend most of the summer growing new leaves and stalks; the same plant in a container only an inch or two larger around than the roots need will produce more bloom.

Allow vegetable and annual flowers somewhat less space than you would in the ground. If the package directions say six inches apart, try them at three to four inches, thinning later if the planting is too close.

If you are transplanting to a larger container, the new soil to make up for the extra size should be apportioned between bottom and sides so the actual level of the surface soil over the roots remains the same. An unsharpened pencil can be used as a tamp to firm it as much as the old soil is. The new soil, ideally, should be of the same texture and consistency as the old. If not, it is probably better to start afresh by shaking and washing all the old soil from the roots, and repotting entirely with fresh.

Place a stone or piece of broken clay pot over the drainage hole to prevent its being plugged with soil. Pour in soil while holding the plant at a height suitable to the old level stain mark on the stem. This should be down several inches from the lip of the container to allow for watering.

As you add soil, tamp lightly. Try to keep the roots spread out and down in a natural manner. Cut out any girdling roots, and any blackened tips (usually the result of over-watering).

Peatlite is very spongy and needs a fair amount of tamping but it will never be as tight and dense as mixtures containing soil.

Peatlite and most other soil mixtures can be used from year to year, although it is usually a good idea to take off the top few inches and add some fresh. But we have citrus trees indoors, and spruce out, both in the same mixture after five years, with only the new soil added as we repot larger from time to time. (High, leafy plants that catch the wind are better in heavier soil mixes which hold the container down.)

4-8. Planting Wire Baskets, Double Potting

If you have never planted a hanging wire basket before, one of the great mysteries of gardening is how to get the soil to stay in place. The secret lies in buying some uncut sphagnum moss from a floral supplier or a florist. (It is commonly used to keep cut flower stem ends moist, to pack around bare-root nursery stock, etc.)

Soak the moss and fit sheets of it into the bottom of the basket, and then around the

To plant in wire baskets, first line them with uncut sphagnum moss, add some soil and continue the lining process.

sides. When you have the first circular layer on, put in some potting soil so it holds the moss in place but doesn't come to its top. Then apply another layer around the side, again adding more soil, until the moss sticks up above the top wire. It can then be folded over. Start with damp potting mixture, then add a little more moisture before planting. If the basket is big and you want a little more water reserve, use double layers of moss.

Using a similar technique, small and medium clay pots that normally dry out too quickly can be double potted, using a size-larger pot for the outside. Line the bottom with uncut moss, making sure the drainage hole is clear. Use enough moss so the two pot rims are level. Then feed sheets of moss around the sides and down until it is packed so the inside pot is tight in the other one. This acts as a reservoir and also helps reduce loss of water by evaporation through the sides.

You can apply the same idea to a decorative planter with a plant in a clay pot in the center. By packing either uncut or ordinary brown peat moss around, under and over the pot surface, you can reduce the amount of watering needed, and at the same time give the plant the appearance of being planted in the container.

If you intend to use an outer container without external drainage, use a separate pot for the plant and sit it inside on small pebbles or pieces of broken pot. Check inside periodically to make sure the water level is below the bottom of the pot, and drain as necessary.

4-9. Fertilizing

No matter how rich the soil you start with, it will soon run out of soluble minerals plants need for healthy growth. Growing plants in containers is extremely intensive cultivation; the necessary frequency of watering alone will dissolve minerals and carry them out of the reach of roots. So a regular program of using fertilizer is necessary.

It is possible to make do with the pellet-type fertilizer that most home gardeners have on hand for lawn and flowers. But you'll be guessing at the amount needed and the chances are the plant will get too much or too little by whim.

It is much safer, easier, and more scientific to use an instantly soluble high analysis fertilizer powder (that also contains trace elements) at the recommended dilution rate. This is safe at one teaspoon (level measuring spoon) to a quart of water, one tablespoon to a gallon.

Once plants have been growing in new potting soil for six to eight weeks, start using the dilute solution in place of normal watering once every one to two weeks over the growing season.

There are various formulas that help produce green growth, flowering and fruiting. But a good standard one also suitable to house plants in winter has a ratio of 20:20:20. Buy the cheapest brand you can find, no matter what advertising claims are made for more expensive kinds. The basic ingredients are all the same and may come from the same manufacturer.

This is an all-purpose ratio. If you wish to vary it you could alternate applications using a grade 10:52:17 or 10:45:15 for root and fruit crops and summer annual flowers. One firm has a product it calls "Geranium Food" with a ratio of 15:30:15 which is both inexpensive and good.

Never let the dry powder come in contact with any part of the plants and don't sprinkle it on the soil surface undiluted. However, at the dilution rate recommended, the solution will not harm plants or foliage. Soluble fertilizer can be dissolved at the same rate in an insecticide-fungicide spray which will then both feed the leaves and protect against pests.

4-10. Watering

Again, because of the relatively small size of the containers, the fact that they sit up above the soil line, and that they likely catch very little rain, watering is critical.

There are soil moisture indicators, schemes to use special wicks from inside the pots through the drainage holes down into a central source of either water or fertilizer solution. Some commercial growers have networks of tubes running from a reservoir to each container and water flows out on a timer basis. Various self-watering pots are on the market.

But for most container gardeners, the old finger test is still the rule. Touch the soil on top and just slightly below the surface. If it is dry, it's time to water. Follow the same rule as for house plants indoors: apply enough so some runs out the bottom into the drip tray. Let the plant stand in the runoff for 10 or 15 minutes, drain and replace. This guarantees that the central rootball will get wet, too — potbound plants sometimes let water run right past at first but then gradually reabsorb what's in the drip tray.

On hot dry summer days when the wind is blowing you may need to water before and after going to work. On cool, wet days, once a week may be enough. Water on demand, not on schedule.

Container plants are a problem during vacations. Handy types may be able to arrange a planter box with a false bottom and wicks leading to a water supply below. Plants may be enclosed for short periods in plastic bags so long as they are out of the sun and the leaves do not touch the plastic. Pots can be set into the garden soil on stones and mulched over their surface — this works particularly with red clay which can absorb moisture through the sides. Drip trays will hold enough for a few days.

But the best solution is probably to arrange with a neighbor to check and water periodically during your absence. Particularly valuable plants need special attention and you may want to take one or two with you.

If you have extra plants in the garden, or a source for them, annual flower planters can be left alone to take their chances. If they survive, so much to the good, if not, replace them on your return.

4-11. Repotting

Plants that grow all year in containers will need repotting occasionally. Don't do this frequently, or as an annual rite, since you don't want to encourage great growth which will make the plant unmanageable. Most hardy evergreens and trees, and tropical evergreens indoors, can go for two to five years in the same pot. But when the plant is obviously potbound with little or no growth, and roots coming out the drainage holes, move it on to a container one size larger. This means, on the average, about one or at the most two inches bigger across the mouth. Do not take a little plant and put it into a huge container alone. In cold, wet weather it will suffer from waterlogged roots and may die.

Repotting larger should be done in spring or early summer when a new flush of growth takes place. But renewing soil on the surface of the pot can be done any time, except for large planters that have spent the winter uncovered. On these, remove two to six inches of soil and replace with fresh before planting for the season.

4-12. Wintering Plants

Tender perennials, house plants and tropical or semi-tropical evergreens, tuberous begonias, caladiums, fuchsias and similar types should be brought indoors before the furnace goes on regularly so they can get used to heated indoor conditions with drier air gradually.

Some kinds, such as wax begonias, geraniums, lantana and impatiens, become too big outdoors to grow comfortably on window sills over winter. It is better to take cuttings of them in August to root. Grow the young plants indoors and discard the old parents. The young plants will become mature over fall and early winter. Then you can take more cuttings to root for the outdoor containers next summer.

Hardy trees, shrubs and evergreens cannot spend the winter indoors. They need the cold, dormant season. Many nurseries keep their stock over winter tipped on their sides after freeze-up, but they will do well upright so long as they go into freeze-up well supplied with moisture. Moving them to a north or east exposure where they are shaded from the winter sun and where they get some wind protection will help prevent browning of the foliage, and increase their chances of survival. But do not wrap them in an air-tight plastic bag which only increases the chances of sun burning. Burlap is safe.

If there is a prolonged winter thaw, check to be sure the soil is still damp, watering if necessary. Light, fluffy snow won't hurt them, but keep them away from the drip line of eaves or any place where slush or ice will fall or be shovelled on them.

5 Training Climbing Plants

Plants that climb or can be trained to fences, walls, pillars, arbors or other upright support add an extra dimension to the garden. They can roof a patio against the sun, provide a screen for privacy, decorate and soften the lines of an upright pillar or wall, and make use of a small plot of ground so you can grow more things in a garden with no room to spare.

5-1. Annual Vines

Annual vines — those that can be grown from seed to maturity in one season — mentioned in the previous chapter are also possible subjects for gardens in the ground. They are all frost-tender and don't even do well in cold ground, so they should either be started in containers early indoors to set in the ground later, or be bought as started plants. Those with hard seed coats need nicking before the seed is sown to speed germination.

Some cling by twining, as morning glory does, and need a thin support such as string or wire. Others, such as sweet peas, have clinging tendrils separate from the growing tip; these may be supported on heavier uprights, such as a wooden trellis or thin stakes set against a wall or fence.

Sweet peas do well against a piece of chicken wire between two stakes set along or against another fence or a wall. Unlike most annual vines, they resist cold and frost and the seeds should be sown quite early — as soon as the ground can be worked. Plant them in a trench of topsoil over a four-inch to six-inch layer of compost or rotted manure, preferably in full sun. Plants should be about a foot apart. They will generally train themselves to the wire, but any that don't can be held in place with string.

Annuals are fast-growing and relatively shallow-rooted. They need a ready supply of soil moisture and soluble minerals. Liquid fertilizer applied every couple of weeks and regular watering when rains fail will help them produce flowers till frost. Most annual vines do better in quite warm weather, but sweet peas, the exception, produce better when the weather is cool.

Annual vines are self-limiting, of course, because frost cuts them down. All the gardener has to do is remove the dead stems from the supports, and remove the supports themselves if they are temporary, such as strings.

5-2. Hardy, Woody Vines

Because they are going to be in place a long time, hardy, perennial vines need better ground preparation than annuals. Plant them as you would plant shrubs (Chapter 1). Generally vines require less root run for the amount of top they produce.

Vines have several ways of clinging and it's a good idea to know which is which before planting. Clematis and grapes, for example, cling by twining shoots that wrap themselves around whatever is handy. Others, like euonymus, Boston ivy, English ivy, Virginia creeper and climbing hydrangea, develop rootlike developments with discs or short shoots that attach themselves to flat surfaces. A third group supports itself by a trunk that twists round in a circle repeatedly as it grows. Examples are Dutchman's pipe, bittersweet, wisteria and climbing honeysuckle. Moreover, these twining kinds vary as to whether they twine from left to right, or vice versa. Thus it's important to look at the way the vine grows when you try to help it along.

Clinging vines are suitable for brick and stone, but not usually to frame construction where their suction cups or rootlets may penetrate, and where the vine has to be removed when it comes time to paint. Twining vines, on the other hand, if grown to aluminum or copper wire, can be taken down and laid on the ground when house repairs are necessary without losing the vine.

Fast-growing vines like bittersweet and wisteria should be planted with caution unless you are prepared to be vigilant with the pruning shears. Left alone they soon become a tangle of shoots and leaves and may even damage roofs and eaves. Wisterias, though, may be grown to one trunk with shoots pruned back severely each year. Eventually the trunk becomes self-supporting. If several shoots come out from the roots, they can be allowed to twine around each other. Eventually they get larger and become woody, creating the effect of a woven trunk.

Grapes, which cling by tendrils and are grown on wires for commercial and home production of fruit, may also be grown on arbors, on supports for patio roofs, and simply on fences. If they are used mainly for ornament, they only need pruning to keep them in bounds. Trimming back hard on the last year's growth will result in better fruit production.

All fast-growing vines can be trained over a wire fence to give it the appearance of a hedge. Virginia creeper is particularly suited to a low brick or stone wall. Boston ivy will cling to and cover an old, naked tree stump that was cut high. A number of vines will climb downpipes and tree trunks. But some will damage live trees: a safe vine to use for this purpose is climbing hydrangea.

Many home gardeners are afraid to grow clinging vines even on masonry houses for fear they will damage the brick. There may indeed be some damage over a long period of time, but one need only look at the ancient buildings in Europe and the United Kingdom with ivies grown there for hundreds of years to realize that the damage in one person's lifetime is minimal.

So far we've been talking about deciduous vines (those that drop their leaves in winter). An evergreen wall climber is a sometime thing in the northern climates except for south coastal British Columbia where *Euonymus vegetus* selections, English ivy, *Clematis paniculata*, Henry's and Hall's honeysuckles, and *Akebia quinata* are either evergreen or semi-evergreen, keeping their leaves in mild winters. In not-quite-so-mild areas, English ivy may be evergreen in mild winters on north or east walls; only *Euonymus vegetus* varieties are reliably so.

5-3. Clematis Best for Flowers

Of all the vines that produce flowers (apart from the annuals), clematis is probably the most spectacular, with many named varieties. They are easy to grow in soil that is alkaline, cool and well drained.

Clematis needs its leaves in the sun so it is an ideal vine where shade falls on the ground but shines through higher up on a trellis, arbor, fence or wall. It climbs by tendrils and needs strings or wires for best support. It also tends to send out a great many shoots; continued and severe pruning is needed to produce the largest flowers. Indeed, an old vine will send out so many shoots that, if left unchecked, it becomes a tangled mess of foliage and tendrils that are impossible to separate.

In severe climates clematis dies back to the snowline, which doesn't hurt at all. Even where this doesn't happen the plant will benefit from being pruned that way before new growth appears in spring.

These comments apply to Clematis Jackmani, the most popular species with named varieties and hybrids such as Nelly Moser, Ramona, Gypsy Queen, Ernest Markham. They bloom on new shoots produced each spring, as do *paniculata* and *tangutica*. There are other kinds that bloom on wood produced the summer before, so if you're in doubt check with your supplier. Such clematis should be pruned after bloom.

Other perennial vines with attractive flowers include *Hydrangea petiolaris*; flowering honeysuckles with fragrant blooms in colors from white to scarlet and including a bi-color — dropmore scarlet is hardy on the prairies; Chinese matrimony vine with purple flowers; and, of course, wisteria where hardy.

NOTE: English ivy may be used as a ground cover as it tends to root at nodes. It may be clipped at the edges of the plot to be covered, or allowed to climb a wire fence where it will grow through and up. By clipping this you can turn it into a hedge. It will retain its leaves when covered with snow but lose them above ground although its stems are winter hardy in moderate climate areas.

5-4. Climbing Roses Don't Climb

Climbing roses are not true climbers at all. They produce elongated shoots very swiftly in one season and may reach heights of 20 or 30 feet in climates where the canes do not freeze back. But these long, arching shoots are not self-supporting and if left to their own devices, even when grown against a trellis or pillar, will bend over to the ground where they'll form a thicket by rooting at the tip and starting a new plant.

Pillars, ramblers and climbing forms of other roses, such as hybrid teas, are spectacular in bloom, but far more trouble than most other plants treated as climbers. To look and perform best they need not only fertilizer and extra water over the summer, but also regular spraying and, in colder climates, winter protection. This will vary from hilling soil over the base as insurance against a deep freeze that might kill the tall canes, to removing canes from their support and covering them with earth in areas where deep freezes are normal each winter.

Nevertheless climbing roses are spectacular in bloom, and provide reliable color over the season if you plant repeat bloomers. In colder areas avoid climbing hybrid teas which are no more cold hardy than the non-climbing types.

Climbing roses that bloom only once a year in early summer should be pruned just after bloom fades by removing the oldest, woodiest canes, at or below, ground level. To keep the plant the same size, allow as many new shoots to grow up as you removed. Let the plant get bigger by allowing more to grow, or reduce it by letting fewer stay. These new shoots may also be removed with sharp pruning shears at ground level or where they originate on a main stem. Dead wood should be removed any time.

Since new shoots grow so vigorously it is sometimes difficult to tell if they are the desired variety or a sucker or wild shoot from the root-stalk. If the rose is on its own roots, there's no problem. If it is grafted, check the origin of the shoot. If it comes from any part of the bud union which appears as a bump on the stem, or from above it, it is okay. If it comes from below remove it at the source. The old test based on whether or not it has seven leaflets to a leaf is not reliable. However, a rose may still be saved even though you've let a lot of sucker shoots grow, so long as the bud union is alive and has at least one live cane. If not, discard the rose.

A rambler rose is spectacular in bloom, but far more trouble to grow and maintain than most other plants treated as climbers.

5-5. Turning other Plants into Climbers

If you get interested in covering walls, fences, garages, arbors and other supports with plants, you may want to experiment with other kinds. For it is possible to grow a number of non-climbing trees and shrubs in a flat manner against a surface that will support it, or to train arms out side-ways along a wire or board fence.

Climbing roses may be trained this way to form patterns against a wall, but their thorns make working with them painful so you tend to neglect the regular pruning necessary.

Firethorn (*Pyracantha*) is a colorful shrub with white flowers and bright orange berries that lends itself to training against a wall. You could, for example, keep a central trunk and allow side branches to start. Train these in a straight line out from the trunk. Space the branches by pinching out unwanted shoots to form a regular horizontal pattern.

Or you could start from the base, pinching out the central shoot 18 inches above the ground, and allowing a number of branches to grow. Tie them to the wall so they radiate like the ribs of a fan. Cut off all unwanted shoots, and cut the ends off the wanted ones when they reach the length you want.

Virtually any shrub that is hardy in your area can be trained in this manner, but vigorous ones that put out plenty of foliage, and preferably have either colorful leaves, flowers or fruit, are most decorative.

There is not nearly so wide a choice of

evergreens, many of which are either too slow-growing or do not readily put out new shoots from old wood (which eliminates spruce and pine). Eastern and western juniper (red cedar) are good subjects since they are relatively fast-growing and are available in varieties with colorful foliage. They also bear blue fruit.

5-6. Fruit Trees a Good Choice

Fruit trees lend themselves easily to growing against a wall and in fact trained fruit trees have been grown for centuries in Europe and Asia. As a result, a number of patterns of training their branches have become established. These are called espalier, cordon, fan, pyramid, bush, gridiron, oblique cordon, twin cordon, upright cordon, and triple and double U cordon.

In any case, you must start with either a young grafted tree (dwarfs are easier to handle and suitable for low walls, but grow more slowly and in general are less vigorous), or a tree whose training has been started by a nurseryman.

You need a sunny wall, fence or other support, and well-prepared planting area. If you are starting the training yourself, buy a young, grafted nursery tree and cut off the trunk some six to 36 inches above the graft, depending on how low you want the first branches to appear. Dormant side buds should then begin to grow. You tie these along wires fastened to the wall or to a framework made out in the pattern you want. Everytime a twig grows longer than a foot, cut it back to the stems fastened to the wires.

Espalier shape consists of a central trunk from which side branches are trained out horizontally in balanced pairs. There may or may not be a piece of trunk sticking up in the center.

A cordon is made by having only two side, horizontal branches coming from an abbre-viated trunk. An oblique cordon may consist of a single trunk grown to the right or left at an angle from the upright, or it may consist of an upright trunk with branches on one side only, and these grown at an angle upwards.

A twin cordon looks like a U, with a short central trunk and two upright branches about a foot apart and joined at the bottom. A triple cordon looks like two U's together, both sharing one upright: a trunk with an upright on either side joined together at the bottom. A double U cordon starts out like a double cordon, but when the two side branches start growing upright, they are pinched to induce two more shoots each to develop, each pair of which is grown like a U, giving a candelabra effect.

The fan shape is self-explanatory, a chosen number of branches being trained outward from the brief trunk (a bush form is similar except that the plant is grown free-standing, away from the wall).

To get a pyramid type, side branches are pinched to induce them to branch in turn so that small fans appear opposite each other on either side of the main trunk at designated intervals, perhaps three or four groups of them per plant. A gridiron is like three triple cordons inside each other with a central trunk up the middle.

But there is no rule that says you have to follow these patterns exactly. You can train your fruit tree to follow the lines you want, or to make up for an uneven structure, such as, for example, a fence that steps down or up. You could allow the trunk to start up below a window, and then train the branches to go out, and around, and up the sides of the window.

A diamond pattern can be created with a number of trees planted in a row and their branches angled left and right to cross each other. Pears are grown this way against a wall of the United Nations building in New York. The effect is eye-catching and, curiously, the crossing branches have grafted so that in effect all the separate trees share the same sap.

Once the trained tree has taken on the shape you want – training has to be done with

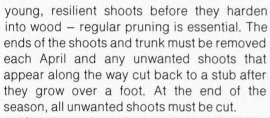

In winter, wrap sapling trees from root level to lowest limb to prevent drying of wood tissue, sunscald and borer damage.

After wrapping, the top can be thinned by pruning. Remove lateral or inside branches, not ends of branches.

young, resilient shoots before they harden into wood — regular pruning is essential. The ends of the shoots and trunk must be removed each April and any unwanted shoots that appear along the way cut back to a stub after they grow over a foot. At the end of the season, all unwanted shoots must be cut.

After the early spring pruning, wait till the first flush of the new season's growth is over, probably late in June. Then remove the shoots that are a foot long, but only back to a base pair of leaves so that any fruit spurs that may grow will remain. All the shorter twigs should grow on. Pruning trained trees requires a balance be kept between keeping them to shape and allowing enough leaves to remain to manufacture food.

This pruning pattern is repeated through the summer, at the end of which all leafy twigs are removed except the terminal ones (which come off in spring).

At the same time the plant must have available moisture and minerals. All trained trees and dwarf trees in particular are more susceptible to drought than unpruned ones whose roots will be more extensive.

Apply either chemical fertilizer or barnyard manure over the root area once a year, the manure in fall, the chemical fertilizer in spring. Dilute fertilizer solution may be used in place of normal watering from time to time if the plant seems to need a boost, or if the leaves are pale. Sprays should be used to protect against insects and disease just as for any other fruit tree (see Chapter 7).

Apples and pears and crabapples are as satisfactory as any for the training technique, but it is also possible to use peaches, plums, nectarines and cherries. Grapes may also be trained in these ways as well as in the conventional cordon on wire, or over a trellis. And any of the designs described here could be the basis for training non-fruiting plants described earlier.

Apples and pears will not fruit well, if at all, in heavily shaded locations. Peaches are more tolerant. But all will do better on a minimum of six hours of direct sunlight a day. A location with sun till noon is actually better for peaches, which bloom early. They are subject to late frosts and the heat of the afternoon sun tends to bring the bloom ahead.

Growing plants to walls and fences not only enhances them, but allows you to grow your own fruit without using up garden space.

All the pruning effectively dwarfs the fruit trees rather drastically so that they will not produce as much as open-grown trees. But the individual fruit are larger, juicier, and by all accounts better-tasting.

Maintaining and Fertilizing Lawns and Gardens

You can't grow a good vegetable, flower or shrub garden by letting nature take its course. We don't think there would be any serious argument about that. Almost everyone knows that the result would be a weedy field.

But many home gardeners think all they have to do to a lawn is cut it (reluctantly) when it gets too long. In fact, the care you put into a lawn will show up immediately in the quality of grass you get as a result. A lawn is a garden, too, and a first quality lawn requires as much care as a first quality flower garden.

Growing a thick, rich lawn is another form of intensive gardening where a great many grass plants are growing close together. To keep them that close and growing vigorously, it is necessary to supply extra moisture when rains fail (as they frequently do in the summer), and to supply extra minerals in soluble form. (Growing a thick, rich lawn that stays green all summer goes against the natural cycle in a continental climate where grass grows vigorously in spring, rushes to flower and seed, then goes dormant and brown until fall rains bring on a late growth before frost.)

A first class lawn starts with the soil in which the grass plants are growing (described in Chapter 7 of Volume 8), and if you are working with an old lawn there is not much you can do about the soil immediately, short of tilling the old grass under and starting afresh.

But there is a great deal you can do about

supplying extra water and soluble minerals. Set up a schedule of applying fertilizer according to the degree of luxuriant lawn you want, and according to your climate area (long or short).

For a luxuriant lawn and in a relatively long-season area, apply fertilizer five times over the growing season. Apply it three times for a moderately luxuriant lawn and in short-season areas. Two applications a season produce a reasonable turf with grass plants spaced somewhat further apart. One application a year is better than nothing and will help grass plants become sturdier than if they got no fertilizer at all.

6-1. Working Out a Program

Using the formula described in Chapter 3 of Volume 8, take a fertilizer ratio and divide the first figure, which represents the percentage of nitrogen, into 100 to get the amount of fertilizer in pounds that should be spread evenly over each 1,000 square feet of lawn space.

Because grass is a green, leafy grower, and we are not looking for grain or fruit from it, we use a fertilizer that has a high first figure.

Examples are 10:6:4, 20:10:5, 12:4:8, 20:5:5 and so on. For each 1,000 square feet, you'd use 10 pounds of the first, five pounds of the second, eight to nine pounds of the third and five pounds of the last on each application. By working out the cost of the fertilizer per pound and then multiplying by the number of pounds you need, you can shop around for best fertilizer prices, which are escalating due to the oil situation and world shortages.

In addition, there are materials such as urea (45:0:0) and ammonium nitrate (34:0:0) which have very high percentages of nitrogen, but no phosphorus or potash. These must not be used — dry — on any lawn when it is in active growth, although they may be scattered lightly over a frozen lawn in early spring before new growth has begun as the first, pre-season fertilizer application. If you do use these materials, apply 2-1/2 to three pounds of urea or three to five pounds of ammonium nitrate per 1,000 square feet.

So far we've been describing fertilizers that provide soluble minerals. There are also premium-priced products that have up to 3/4 of the nitrogen in a slowly-soluble form, described as "slow-release", "long-feeding", or "UF" (for urea-formaldehyde). These have the advantage in warm weather of slowing down the dissolving of the nitrogen and thus feeding over a longer period rather than all at once. They are useless in cold weather, as are natural organics such as dehydrated manures and sewage sludges. These require bacterial action to release their minerals, and bacteria are not active in cold soils, such as in early spring when you want to give your grass a boost.

6-2. For a Luxuriant Lawn

So the first application of fertilizer should be, ideally, before the grass turns green in climates with a winter freeze-up (apply in late winter where grass remains green all winter).

This should be a high-nitrogen, soluble mineral product, with a high first figure, as described, or a nitrogen-only product (urea or ammonium nitrate). Buy by price; the cheapest product will do the same job as the most expensive.

If the application is made on frozen ground, or on top of a light covering of snow, there is no need to water immediately after. If the grass has already turned green and begun to grow, arrange to apply the fertilizer just before a rainfall, or irrigate after application.

You can broadcast fertilizer by hand over small areas without danger of uneven application if you follow the instructions for broadcasting grass seed in two parts. You can also use a fertilizer cart (being careful not to stop with the feeder gate open, to make turns evenly, and not to refill it on the grass but on a sheet of paper or plastic) or a circular spreader.

This first application will stimulate the grass into vigorous growth as soon as the soil gets above 35° at the root level, and should carry it for up to two months. The 15th of May is a good marker date for the second application, and this time it is worth the extra price to get a slow-release fertilizer so the grass will have a ready supply of minerals fairly evenly for the next few weeks.

Near the end of June, use a slow-release fertilizer once again. Cut the grass first, then apply the fertilizer evenly, and let the sprinkler run for at least 15 minutes over the whole area, longer if the ground is dry (see watering below).

Grass naturally slows its growth dramatically in hot weather. Fertilizing during July and August will mostly benefit weeds and may actually harm the grass, so wait until Labor Day for the next application. Again use a slow release type.

Make the final application around early October. This time the aim is to strengthen the roots of the grass plants so they will be in good shape for winter. And this time, as in early spring, there is no point in using a slow-release product. You could use 7:7:7 (or similar formula) or one of the so-called winter feeders with a larger last figure, indicating it has more potash for winter hardiness. The latter is especially good on sandy soils, but not necessary on clays or on the prairies where soils are naturally high in potash.

If you fertilize three times a year, begin with the slow-release application around the middle of May, repeat near the end of June, and then apply the last around Labor Day.

If you fertilize twice a year, make the first in late May and the last around Labor Day. On a single annual application, distribute the fertilizer some time between Labor Day and early October, using a 7:7:7 or winter feeder-type product, or simply use a general garden fertilizer, judging the amount by dividing the first figure into 100 as indicated.

6-3. Watering the Lawn

As with fertilizing, watering a lawn on a regular schedule will produce a thicker, deeper green turf than would nature left to itself. But the two must be in conjunction: Watering alone will simply wash soluble minerals below the grass root level; fertilizing without irrigation is likely to cause soluble minerals to become too concentrated in the soil.

An unwatered lawn will survive droughts and heat waves by going dormant and turning brown. And that is not what we have come to expect from a lawn. But by supplementing nature we can get around that trend to dormancy.

This means applying a regular amount of water as the soil under the grass dries out; it does not mean keeping the grass soaking wet. Nor does it mean a light sprinkling after dinner as an entertainment. Grass needs the wet-dry cycle as do most other plants.

One inch of water is the amount that will wet average soils to a depth of six inches, about as far down as most grass roots penetrate. It will take less water to penetrate sandy soils that deeply, more water for clays. In average summer weather without rain, the soil will dry again in a week to 10 days (sooner for sands; later for clays). So the program is to apply enough water evenly over the whole lawn area so that all plants get water to their root tips (rainfall plus irrigation) as soon as the soil becomes dry at the six-inch-deep level.

The exact timing is not critical. It won't hurt if you apply the water before the soil is dry at the six-inch-deep level. And you can probably keep the grass from going dormant if you water a little after it's dry six inches down. But there are ways to tell: lawn grasses tend to get a glassy, slightly bluish look just before they wilt from dryness. That's the time to water.

How do you know when you've watered enough? If you are satisfied to apply the average one inch, mark the inside of a straight-sided can with nailpolish at one inch from the bottom. Set the can at various spots (or use several cans). Time the sprinkler to see how long it takes to put one inch of water in the cans at the place where the sprinkler pattern is lightest. From then on simply run the sprinkler that amount of time.

A simpler test is to run the hose long enough until either water stands on the surface of the lawn, or until the earth under the grass is soft and squishy. Then don't water again until the glassy look appears.

You can supplement light rainfalls by running the sprinkler the next day. If you want to be precise you can measure the rainfall with a marked straight-sided can, as suggested above. But growing lawns is not an exact science and there is plenty of leeway in nature. Just remember to give the grass a chance to dry out between soakings.

Grass growing over the roots of shrubs, hedges and trees, expecially if they are surface-rooted kinds, will be competing for moisture. You can compensate by watering (and fertilizing) twice as often in such areas.

6-4. How Mowing Affects the Lawn

A plot of grass is obviously not a lawn if it isn't mowed. But the cutting off of the tops of the grass blades benefits the gardener rather than the grass, since grass roots grow down

Cut at the proper height of two inches, grass blades will shade out many weed seedlings and prevent other sprouting weed seeds from ever getting in contact with the soil.

into the soil at a depth proportionate to how long the blades are allowed to grow. Close mowing means shallow roots and susceptibility to sun, heat and drought as well as to winter damage. Closely-mowed grass will suffer more from foot traffic and be more open and thus subject to weed infestation. It requires more maintenance to keep it healthy and relatively thick. (Creeping bent, a grass unsuitable to home lawns, does withstand very close mowing, but succeeds only with extremely heavy maintenance and daily attention.)

So don't cut grass at the one-inch level. At 1-1/2 inches you're allowing it a little more vigor. But a two-inch cutting height is better. This is long enough for adequate food production, and to provide shade over the soil surface in hot weather. It allows the roots to grow six inches deep, which makes them relatively heat- and cold-proof. At two inches, grass blades will shade out many weed seedlings, including crab grass, and prevent other sprouting weed seeds from ever getting in contact with the soil.

Frequency of mowing affects the vigor of the grass as well. If you let growth go unchecked until it is four or five inches tall, then wade in with a mower and slash it back, consider what has happened to the grass. It

was adjusting to more and more food-making leaf surface and then suddenly has it reduced by half or less.

On the other hand, frequent mowing whenever the grass gets slightly above the two-inch level is little or no shock at all. The plants adjust to a relatively constant two inches of blade. Frequent mowing has an advantage to the gardener as well. It produces fine, short clippings that can remain where they fall, and never become a nuisance on the grass surface (balls of heavy, wet clippings spewed out by rotary mowers should be removed).

In fact, by letting fine clippings remain to dry and sift down among the grass plants where they act as a mulch and eventually decay to add to the topsoil, you are letting the grass itself supply the equivalent of one feeding a year.

6-5. Weeding Is Important

While vigorous, thick turfs cut at two inches or higher are relatively resistant to weed infestations, there are so many weed seeds blowing around from careless neighbors, vacant lots or fields nearby that sooner or later some weeds will appear in what was once a weed-free lawn. These can be cut out below the ground surface by using a V-type weed tool, or by spot spraying with a combination weedkiller — a combination is more effective on resistant and narrow-leafed weeds than a single herbicide used alone. If the lawn is maintained as suggested for luxury lawns, it should not need overall spraying.

However, in renovating an old, thin lawn, overall spraying may be the only way. In this case, choose a windless, sunny day with the temperature just over 70°. Spray carefully, and close to the ground so the spray will not drift on to nearby plants which it can severely damage. Herbicides are more effective if applied a day or two after the lawn has been fertilized and watered. Tough old perennial weeds, and persistent narrow-leafed ones,

An unweeded, unfertilized lawn is an eyesore.

such as knotweed, may require one or more repeat treatments.

6-6. Aerating

Lawns that take a lot of foot traffic, old lawns that need renovating and any lawn grown in a heavy clay soil will benefit from periodic aerating. This requires holes to be punched in the soil two to four inches deep with a spike arrangement — a spiked wheel or a tamper-type with spikes driven through a piece of board attached to a handle — or a machine that removes plugs of soil. The coring machine does a better job in opening up the soil since it leaves a cleanly cut hole; the spikes merely compress the soil around the hole.

But either method helps open up the soil to let rain, air and fertilizer enter the root area. It eventually makes the soil more spongy to the benefit of the grass roots.

Commercial maintenance firms will provide this service for a fee, or you can rent or make a machine and do it yourself. If you do, soak the lawn several times to make it soft and spongy, or better still, aerate in spring just as the frost is coming out of the ground (otherwise keep foot traffic off the lawn until it firms up again).

A core-removing machine leaves the plugs on the surface of the ground, which is a little untidy at first. If they bother you, rake them off and put them on the compost pile. Otherwise they will break down quickly under spring rains.

6-7. Top-Dressing

Top-dressing is a time-honored English lawn-making custom that gives you the feeling you are really doing something to make the lawn grow better. In fact, it is an expensive time-waster and benefits your waistline more than the grass. It may even import weeds to your lawn you didn't have before.

It does, admittedly, add a little more soil under the grass as it gradually sifts down. But not much. Loose earth compacts rather quickly to a fraction of its former volume. And the most you should rake over grass without running a risk of smothering it is 1/4 to 1/2 inch. Compact that and what have you got?

You'll get better value for your money by spending it on water and fertilizer and keeping the grass growing vigorously (when it makes it own topsoil with clippings and sloughed-off roots).

However, there is one situation where top-dressing not only pays off, it may be the only way you can keep grass growing — over the surface roots of a large tree. By annual or twice-yearly top-dressing with topsoil or sifted compost you can provide a little soil for the grass roots. It's only a holding measure because the tree's roots take over eventually anyway.

Of course topsoil can be used to fill a hollow, allowing you to reseed on top to level a sunken area of lawn. But ordinarily the best way to fix hollows in the lawn is to strip back the sod, fill the hollows with lightly compacted topsoil, and then relay the sod.

Fix bumps in a reverse manner, peeling back the sod, removing soil and then relaying the sod.

Raking topsoil over the lawn may also be useful in filling tiny holes or hollows, and prior to overseeding, but even then, it is better practice to scarify the lawn with a saw-toothed rake to open the soil and seed directly on to it.

6-8. Rolling

Never roll a lawn with a weighted roller as a matter of course. This only compacts the soil under it. Done in the spring on heavy clay, it may change it to near brick.

An unweighted roller is sometimes useful in pressing back into contact with the soil sod that has been lifted by frost or traffic. It is also helpful when laying new sod. But it can only damage the soil under it if you try to flatten hummocks with it.

6-9. Thatch

Luxury lawns that are heavily fertilized and watered may produce more clippings than can rot in a year and in addition some surface rooting. This build-up of vegetable matter will eventually block air and water from the ground, invite disease and reduce the vigor of the grass. If such a build-up is evident you can reduce or remove it in a number of ways.

Hard raking with an ordinary or scarifying rake will remove a good deal. If this is done as a matter of course each spring before new growth begins, thatch will never accumulate enough to cause a problem.

If it does become a problem, repeat the raking procedure in fall or hire a commercial operator to do this. His machine will take grooves out of the lawn which may upset you at first. But the grooves have the added effect of aerifying the soil, and with a good mainte-nance program the grass will soon fill in again.

Where thatch does occur, it's a good idea to use a grass catcher with the mower. Use the clippings as a mulch around shrubs, flowers or vegetables or mix them thoroughly with other garden waste and compost them.

6-10. Ice Rink Damage

Ice rinks built over grass in the back yard are great for young skaters, but ruinous for the grass. There is a tendency to move the location from year to year to make it easier on the sod. But that just multiplies the problem.

It is simpler and easier to make the rink in exactly the same place each year so that only one area is damaged since it will take about two years for the sod (or newly-seeded area) to come back. After the ice goes in spring, sow perennial ryegrass for a temporary, one-season lawn. This makes an acceptable ground cover that will stand foot traffic in summer.

Repeat the procedure each spring until the time comes to give up the rink. Then till the

ground, level and reseed or lay sod for a new, permanent lawn.

6-11. Fertilizing the Rest of the Garden

Deciduous shrubs and trees produce great quantities of leaves each spring and discard them each fall. If the leaves stayed where they fell the cycle would be complete, and there'd be no need to fertilize. But in our gardens they don't. And unless the woody plants' feeder roots share space with grass that is fertilized, they may be short of soluble minerals.

A root feeder facilitates the job of root soaking and root feeding. The device is attached to a garden hose and plunged full depth into the ground.

Since they produce a lot of green growth suddenly in spring, a lawn-type fertilizer is useful to help them along. This could be one of the ratios suggested under lawns, or another where the first figure was larger than the other two. Use one with a high last figure as well, if you are gardening in sand.

It used to be suggested that holes be drilled as deep as 18 inches in the ground under the branches of trees. But studies of tree root behavior have shown that most minerals are absorbed in the top 12 inches of topsoil, perhaps most in the top six inches. So the best (and easiest) way to fertilize is to scatter the material evenly over the area occupied by the roots from about 18 inches from the trunk on large trees to well beyond the branch spread, but especially at the branch tips — this area is known as the "drip line" (where rain drips down) and contains a larger than usual number of feeder roots.

You can use the standard lawn measuring formula, that is, divide the first figure into 100 and spread that amount in pounds over 1,000 square feet (see Section 6-1). Divide by 10 for smaller trees occupying 100 square feet under the branch spread. Apply this amount in early spring and again in early June.

Or you can calculate an amount by the trunk diameter: apply two to three pounds per inch diameter for small trees; give five pounds per inch diameter for large trees. Thus, a tree two feet through would get about 120 pounds of fertilizer per year — in early spring.

It may be difficult to apply this amount without damaging grass or laying it too thick over the roots of the tree if it is growing in a confined space (such as with sidewalk trees). For these, it is easier to use a root feeder with soluble cartridges of fertilizer. Use the feeder repeatedly to get a proper amount of fertilizer to the roots.

In the case of trees confined by pavement, or where many trees and shrubs are growing close together, annual fertilization should be followed. If a tree regains its vigor with fertilization, you could skip a year and see how it is.

Among shrubs, those close to others and especially hedge plants will be more vigorous and leafy with annual spring fertilization.

Calculate the amount to use as for lawns, and broadcast it on the ground over the roots, between and around the plants. A light cultivation of the soil will help it act faster, but don't cultivate deeply or you will only cut off feeder roots.

Most evergreens are quite slow-growing and seldom need more than nature provides if their planting soil was prepared properly. If you feel they need it, scatter a little general garden fertilizer (4:12:10 or similar; 5:10:15 in sands) on the soil from the trunk out just past the branch spread in early spring.

Treat perennial plants and beds the same as for shrubs, except use the general garden ratio suggested for evergreens. For roses, use the calculated amount every month or six weeks from early spring until midsummer, when all feeding should stop.

Treat fruit trees as shade trees, except that the first application in early spring could be ammonium nitrate if you prefer. Fertilize every year for best fruiting. Animal manures, particularly if laden with straw, can be used as a combination fertilizer and mulch, but should not be placed where they touch the trunk. If you cultivate around the trees, do so first and apply the manure afterward.

6-12. Flower and Vegetable Gardens

The intensive cultivation of flower and vegetable gardens not only uses up available minerals, it also exhausts the humus content so more should be added annually. Raw manure or partly worked compost can be dug into the soil in fall (but leave the clods of overturned earth for frost to break up). Well-rotted or dehydrated manure and worked compost (or other form of humus) should be dug into the soil in spring, which is also the time to apply a general garden fertilizer (if you don't use manure).

As before, divide the first figure into 100 and use the answer in pounds for 1,000 square feet. On small gardens use one tenth that amount on 100 square feet and cultivate it in before planting.

After seedlings are well developed, or after transplants have been in place for a month to six weeks, apply an equal quantity of fertilizer again, either broadcast between the rows, or scattered in a circle around individual plants. In dry years this should be watered in thoroughly since plants can't use it until it is in solution.

If you are in doubt as to the amount of fertilizer to use, or can't remember when you last applied it, take the conservative approach. Apply less rather than more.

Individual plants that are not doing well will often respond to an application of dilute fertilizer solution made up by dissolving a teaspoon of soluble 20:20:20 in a quart of water (or a tablespoon in a gallon). This may be sprinkled over foliage and all. It is also useful to increase the size of show blooms, tomatoes, corn cobs, and improve the health of new transplants. Applied through a hose-end spray bottle, it can also help perk up a tired lawn.

7 Specialty Gardens

Once you've actually got your garden planned, planted and growing well you may decide you're especially interested in one aspect of it, or in growing a number of varieties of one kind of plant. It's amazing, for example, how many people who start with one rosebush planted among other shrubs get hooked on roses.

7-1. Roses

Let me admit from the start that there are easier plants to grow than roses. They attract insects and disease. They are not reliably hardy even with winter protection except in mild, maritime areas. And as one wit put it, they are a mighty poor excuse for a shrub. But the flowers they produce make up for all their shortcomings. One of the greatest rewards of gardening is to be able to decorate the house with cut roses from June till killing frost. In fact, one well-grown bush will produce about 30 blossoms a season. Considering their flower size and doubleness, to say nothing of their perfume, that's better than most other garden plants of comparable size.

Roses do best in moderately heavy soils that are slightly acid, although they will get along in sand with humus matter mixed in. Sphagnum peat moss is an ideal amendment

Large hybrid tea rose bushes should be planted at least three feet apart.

to the soil for roses, since it is both acid and high in humus. It could constitute up to one-half the planting mixture (by bulk).

Other factors are essential for success with roses, too. To start they must not be planted where there is poor drainage since they can't tolerate the lack of oxygen in such wet soils. Except in very mild areas, they must be planted deeply, with the bud union two inches below the soil surface as protection against winterkill. They need a minimum of six hours' direct sunlight a day but grow and produce

For healthy roses and good flower production, spray regularly with a combination insecticide-fungicide.

The white floribunda Saratoga roses lining a garden walk add the right touch of color and foliage.

better in full sun. And they must not have root competition from vigorous trees and shrubs. (Given proper spacing, though, they can be grown with other shrubs and evergreens.)

Because of the need to plant the bushes deeply in cold climates, the soil preparation should be done to a matching depth — three feet is not too deep. Strawy barnyard manure (if available), coarse compost, or peat moss sprinkled with general garden fertilizer should be mixed thoroughly with the garden soil. If the subsoil at the bottom of the planting excavation is solid and impervious to water, break it up — weeping tiles may be necessary to provide drainage away from the rose bed. Plant as indicated in Chapter 1.

Just as roses shouldn't have competition from the roots of other plants, so they should not compete with each other, either. Large-growing hybrid tea and grandiflora plants should have a minimum of three feet between them. Smaller-growing hybrid teas and floribundas can be planted as close as 2-1/2 feet if necessary in a small garden.

Spring planting is generally best, but it should be done very early before the rose shows any signs of new growth. If planting can't be done early and new growth has begun, hill soil up around the bush after you've planted it to keep the canes from drying out before the roots establish themselves. Watering is essential for new transplants if rains fail, but never keep them soaking wet.

Early pruning requires removing the smaller of two duplicating or crossing canes, and any canes smaller around than a lead pencil. Cut dead ends of canes back to the nearest live shoot that faces outward from the center of the bush.

Regular spraying with a combination insecticide-fungicide is necessary for healthy roses and good flower production. If you don't wish to use such sprays, or can't maintain a regular schedule, don't try to grow roses. New systemic products that go into the sapstream and are effective for 10 days to several weeks have cut the drudgery out of spraying, but

This semi-circular bed of floribundas serves to break up a large expanse of lawn by adding color.

nothing yet has made roses unattractive to insects and diseases.

Follow fertilizing suggestions in the previous chapter, but remember that roses are planted deeply and it takes some time for fertilizer to work its way down to rose root level. Don't be tempted to double the amount if the first application doesn't bring fast results.

Roses cut in the early morning will last longer in the house, as their stems are turgid with sap. Make the cut just above the highest five-leaflet leaf that faces outward from the center of the bush. (Cutting back to a leaf with fewer leaflets will result in a weaker new shoot.)

Again, in all but milder climates, roses will need considerable winter protection. In some

areas hilling with topsoil to a height of eight to 12 inches over the center of the bush is sufficient. In colder places, you may have to add boxes of leaves or sawdust on top of the soil. In very mild areas where no winter kill happens, a winter mulch of humus is sometimes added.

Fall pruning is not necessary where there will be winterkill — wait till spring to see how far back the canes are dead, and then, as with new plants, cut below that to the topmost shoot facing out. Where there is no winterkill, cut thin canes out and heavy ones back to four or five buds.

7-2. Perennials

Most modern gardeners use perennials intermixed with annuals, shrubs, roses, evergreens as simply another part of the parade of flowers over the season. However, it is still possible to have a garden or border depending only on herbaceous perennials (which die back to the ground in winter, but reappear to flower again the next year). This kind of garden will not be a sheet of color from one end to the other all season. Rather the color will come and go, or move from one end to the other gradually, if the kinds of perennials are arranged that way. Of course a boarder of annuals such as ageratum, sweet alyssum, or dwarf snapdragons can be used for summerlong color, and even spotted here and there among the perennials.

There are hundreds of perennials that can be grown in gardens and the choice is a highly personal one. The following list will provide bloom from the time of the late garden tulips until freeze-up for the small perennial bed.

Garden (German bearded) iris in various colors; geums in reds and yellows; peonies (which need lots of space and support for the flowers); delphiniums (mainly blues but also lavender pink and white; needs staking and will rebloom in September); daylilies (Hemerocallus, various kinds bloom from spring to fall); Lythrum (for damp spots); Oriental poppy; perennial phlox; veronica; perennial asters; chrysanthemums (early, midseason and late).

While some perennials need frequent dividing to keep them in bounds and blooming satisfactorily (iris and delphinium need transplanting every three or four years, daylilies every two or three), many stay a long time in the same place. Peonies in a good location need not be divided or moved for up to 50 years, so the soil in the bed should be thoroughly prepared up to three feet deep. Either keep a mulch on it in summer which will partly break down and improve the soil, or dig humus material in between the plants annually. A winter mulch applied after the ground is frozen will help reduce alternate freezing and thawing and the chance that plants will be heaved out of the ground.

7-3. Lilies

As with perennials, lilies are most often grown in mixed plantings and especially between evergreens where they offer exotic looks, and both color and perfume in summer. But it is possible to have lilies blooming from June till mid-September by choosing among the many kinds available. Thus a lily garden, like a perennial one, will provide its own succession of bloom over the season.

Like roses, lilies need good drainage, and most kinds will only fade in damp or poorly drained locations. If you want to plant lilies and don't have a suitable location, you could create a raised garden or artificial hills.

Like tulips, lilies need deep planting with good earth and a source of nutrients under them. Provide stakes if there is no wind protection. And don't plant them on one side of a building as they bend very strongly to the light. In late fall, plant them one foot deep for winter protection, and to help the bulbs retain flowering size, rather than breaking down into a number of bulblets. The exception is the Madonna lily, which should have no more than two inches of soil over the top of the bulb, and which should be planted or divided in late summer.

Like many other garden subjects, lilies have been extensively hybridised and there are many named varieties, as well as the original species to choose from. Here's a brief list of species and hybrids for a summer of bloom: Wood lily, Golden Chalice hybrids, Elegans, Coral, Star, Madonna, Meadow, Turk's Cap, Hanson, Green Magic, Harlequin, Martagon, Regale, Sentinel, Tiger, Imperial strain, Speciosum.

7-4. Vegetable Gardens

There is satisfaction enough in growing your own food from a patch of ground and this realization even among the high-rise dwellers has brought a new popularity to vegetable gardening, so much so that many municipalities as well as commercial operators, have revived the war-time allotment gardens. Besides the satisfaction of doing the growing themselves, new vegetable gardeners have discovered that their own produce, picked at the peak of size, taste and nutrition, is so far superior to commercial produce there is no comparison.

Commercial varieties are bred to stand rough picking and handling, long trips to market, and long shelf-life. The home gardener is under no such pressure. He can pick it dead ripe and it need keep only long enough to take it to the table. As the old saying has it, put the pot on to boil before you go out to pick the corn. Both corn and garden peas lose up to half their sugar within 24 hours of picking. Tomatoes should be left on the vine till soft and dead ripe. Beans can be picked when tender and young, as may carrots and beets.

Furthermore, the home grower knows exactly what chemical sprays (if any) have been used on the produce about to be eaten, which is quite a comfort. And in these inflationary days, there is sometimes an added and urgent need to reduce the family food bill.

It has been estimated that a garden roughly 30 by 100 feet will produce vegetables in summer worth $80 to $100: if vegetables are consumed not only in summer, but some are

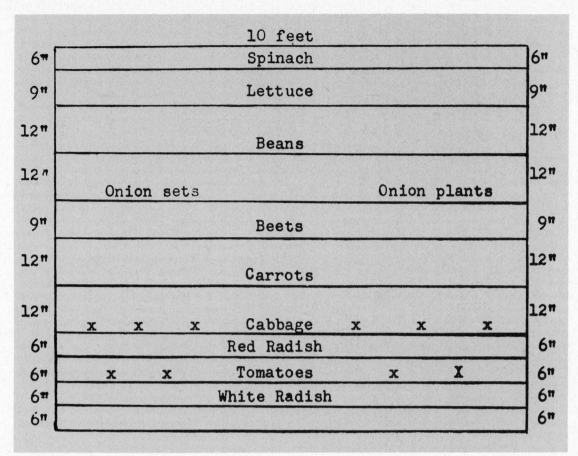

10 feet

6"	Spinach	6"
9"	Lettuce	9"
12"	Beans	12"
12"	Onion sets Onion plants	12"
9"	Beets	9"
12"	Carrots	12"
12"	x x x Cabbage x x x	12"
6"	Red Radish	6"
6"	x x Tomatoes x X	6"
6"	White Radish	6"
6"		6"

Sample layout for a vegetable garden.

canned or frozen for winter, the value of the produce runs $100 to $120 (and prices are going up all the time).

Looking at it another way, a 25 ft. by 100 ft. garden should supply all the vegetables needed by two people over the summer. Or, a 70 by 150-ft. garden should supply enough summer produce for a family of five, plus some to freeze or can.

To grow good produce, and a lot of it in a small space, the soil must be thoroughly prepared, and the humus content renewed annually. Use any handy, nearby source that will provide the humus as cheaply as possible. The minerals can come most easily and cheaply in a bag of fertilizer.

Soil should be prepared as deeply as possible consistent with effort, but the minimum should be one foot (deeper if there is an

Because they are so easy to grow and so productive, snap beans are second in popularity only to tomatoes.

Overplanting and failure to thin are the chief reasons for crops of poor quality. These young people participating in a youth garden program are taught proper thinning and cultivating techniques.

impervious subsoil). Hand digging, followed by hoeing and raking is best the first year; powered rotary tilling works fine from then on. Clots of clay should be broken up or removed; pick the area free of all but tiny stones.

The location of the garden is important in several ways. Ideally it should get full sun all day (although some herbs and leafy vegetables can be grown in part sun). And it should be convenient to a source of water for irrigation during summer droughts. Some garden vegetables (lettuce, celery, onions, cabbage) will do well on a muck soil that tends to be wet, but most prefer a drier location. Sandy, light soils warm up faster in spring, but need more irrigation in summer.

As with flower gardens, tall plants such as corn and tomatoes should be on the north or east end so as not to shade lower-growing vegetables.

Vegetables grow and taste best when they are uninterrupted from start to harvest. Naturally the weather must co-operate, but the gardener can help by making sure water and minerals are available, the soil is of good texture, and that each vegetable plant has enough room to develop properly. Overplanting and failure to thin are the chief reasons for poor quality crops, or downright failures. It is just as important to space plants in the row and space the rows as it is to keep the weeds down.

In large gardens corn is highly valued for its special flavor; potatoes can be grown to supply early new potatoes and even for a winter supply; pumpkins for their decorative value and for Hallowe'en. But they take up too much space in a small garden to be worth it. In little plots, stick to heavy producers like tomatoes, peas, beans, lettuce, onion sets, radishes, and so forth. Use double cropping: replant onion seed, plant radishes to mark rows of other vegetables, plant beans between peas.

Keep on hand an all-purpose vegetable garden spray material in case of invasion by

The grape hyacinth is a hardy bulb of the lily family. (Photo by Malak)

These tall telephone pea vines need support for maximum production.

7-5. Growing Your Own Herbs

Most of the common kitchen herbs are easy to grow if you can give them full sun and well-drained, preferably sandy soil, and if you're willing to weed them. Having your own plot means the herbs are not only handy, but fresh and thus better-tasting.

You can simply try a few plants of several varieties, separating them by simple patterns using bricks, wood, or other material. One common pattern is the wagon wheel, with brick or lumber spokes and rim. The "axle" could have some bright annuals for color, as an herb garden is primarily a green garden.

On a very casual basis, you could simply plant some thyme between patio stones, Dark Opal basil as hedging for the vegetable or flower garden, and dill and sage between other plants or against a foundation wall. Or you could interplant the herbs with annuals to brighten them. Nasturtium would be a good choice since its own leaves are spicy and edible.

On the other hand, if you want to grow a year's supply, allow an area about two feet by four feet for each kind.

Most herbs do well on rather poor, sandy soil that warms up quickly in spring. In most cases a hot location will produce more flavor as well as quicker maturity. If your soil isn't suitable you could build a plot using a good deal of gritty sand and peat moss, or import sandy topsoil.

Harvest early in the morning when flavor is strongest. To dry, cut leaves and stems in dry weather just before the plants flower. Hang the sprigs in bunches in an airy place. Harvest seeds just before they are mature, flower clusters before the buds open and roots as you use them. Many annual herbs are easy to grow from seed. Some are best bought as plants. Horseradish is grown from a piece of root.

Here are some common ones anyone can grow:

● Sweet Basil: Seasoning for soups, tomatoes, salads; annual from seed started

insects — it's virtually impossible to grow cabbage that is edible without using a spray at some time. But check the label and keep the number of days before harvest safety limit in mind.

When the vegetable garden has been harvested, plant ryegrass or ryegrain to hold the soil, provide a green cover and discourage weeds. Turn the soil over, burying the rye, just before freeze-up, but without breaking up the clods. The rye will rot, improving the soil.

indoors or outside after frost danger over.

- Bee or Lemon Balm: Perennial that produces lemon-scented leaves for tea. Buy plants.

- Borage: Flower sprays for cool drinks and salads (also leafy tops); hardy annual to be sown where wanted.

- Caraway: Roots can be eaten as a vegetable, seeds in second year as condiment; a biennial.

- Chervil: Leaves for garnish and French cooking; annual, sow outdoors.

- Chives: Leaves for salads, soups, dressings, egg dishes; hardy perennial from seed or divisions of older plants.

- Coriander: Crushed seeds for flavoring, especially in curry; annual.

- Dandelion: Leaves for salad, flower petals for wine; thick-leaved variety started from seed; plant is perennial.

- Dill: Leaves, flowers and tops for seasoning; seeds for condiments; annual, start outdoors or in pots inside early.

- Florence Fennel: Leaf stalks for fish sauces, seeds and leaves as condiments; annual grown from seed.

- Parsley: Start from seeds soaked in water or root divisions; suitable for pot growing indoors over winter; garnishes for salads, roots for soup; plant is annual or short-lived biennial.

- Rosemary: Young branches in gravies, salads or for tea; tender perennial shrub best kept in pots and brought in over winter.

- Sage: Leaves for seasoning, especially for poultry dressing, or to make tea for sore throats; perennial sub-shrub that is fairly hardy and may live over winter.

- Summer savory: Leaves and young shoots for flavorings and medicinal teas; annual grown from seed.

- Sweet marjoram: Leaves as seasoning, garnish or with spinach; tender perennial grown from seed as an annual.

- Tarragon: Young leaves for salads, pickles, sauerkraut; tender perennial grown as an annual.

- Thyme: Leaves, young stalk and flowering tops as condiments. Perennial that is also useful as ground cover in hot locations where there is no foot traffic.

- Horseradish: Ground root for meat sauce. Propagated from roots. Buy started plants.

7-6. Growing Fruit at Home

In small home gardens, the easiest way to grow fruit is to plant the appropriate shrubs as specimens or part of the shrub border. Currants, Saskatoon serviceberry, high bush cranberry, blueberries (in acid soil – see below) may be interplanted with other shrubs and are attractive enough to hold their own. Raspberries and gooseberries can be used as hedging or as boundary markers. Raspberries are even suitable on a hillside, since plants normally spread through suckers from the roots. Of course these plants may also be grown in rows in a large vegetable garden, or as specimens at one end of a small orchard. But there is no use pretending they don't take up room. If your space is very limited, and they are not your favorite food, pass them by.

Strawberries not only require room, but regular attention as to weeding and removing or transplanting the daughter plants on runners. Beds should be fertilized annually and irrigated when rains fail. And in time, the mature plants will likely develop virus disease and have to be replaced (the bed should be moved to another area). They are not for the

If you have room to plant a row or two of extra bulbs, you'll have flowers for the table without having to cut your display flowers. (Photo by Malak)

Small groups of red tulips and daffodils are planted at intervals along the border of this garden. (Photo by Malak)

tiny garden, nor for anyone who isn't willing to put in the maintenance — an untended strawberry patch soon becomes a jungle of weeds and weed grasses. If strawberries are your fruit, however, we suggest planting the so-called everbearing types which ripen some fruit each month from June and thus spread the season. On the other hand, if you preserve, freeze or make jam, the June-bearers produce more ripe fruit at one time.

Grapes have a limited geographical range and seldom ripen sweet fruit north of it, even if the vines survive. Where they are hardy and ripen fruit, they can be grown on cordons, cut back severely to two buds above the old trunk. In tenderer areas, grow them in a fan shape, taking the vines down in fall, laying them on the ground and covering them with earth for winter protection. Grapes need full sun (as much heat as is possible) and a well-drained, sandy soil into which a good deal of humus has been worked. They respond better to natural organic fertilizers such as barnyard manure.

Of the larger fruit, crabapples are the hardiest. Next come the applecrab hybrids which fruit on the prairies, then apples, pears, peaches and apricots. The latter two are wood-hardy some distance north of their range but their flowers appear early and are susceptible to late spring frosts.

If you are planting fruit trees on a slope, make use of the microclimate in your property by planting peaches on top of the hill and apples on the bottom — cold air flows downhill where frosts are more likely. Similarly, make use of differing soils. Pears, for example, get along nicely on quite heavy clays. Apples prefer a lighter soil, but not so light as peaches which prefer a sandy loam. Sweet cherries also do best on this kind of soil, but sour cherries accept a heavier one except that all cherries need perfect drainage.

Some fruit trees are self-fertile (they can fertilize their own blossoms and produce fruit without there being another tree of the same kind nearby) while others are self-infertile and need a pollinator tree. And there is no clear rule. While most apples are self-fertile, McIntosh, one of the most popular, is usually not. Pears usually need a pollinator tree. Sour cherries are self-fertile; sweet ones are not. Peaches usually are. So are most European plums, although Japanese plums and some hybrids are not. Not only that, if you plant two for pollination, the second plum must be of the same group to do the trick.

Basically, then, except for peaches and sour cherries, it is best to plant two trees of each kind to insure pollination, or persuade your neighbor to plant one. There are nursery trees available, at least among apples and pears, with more than one variety grafted on the same stem which solves the pollination problem in small gardens. And some of these are on dwarfing rootstalks, another distinct advantage.

In fact, it is doubtful if any home gardener should plant a full-size apple or pear tree. They eventually grow to a size that requires step-ladders and power spraying equipment, whereas dwarf trees are available on roots that produce an 8, 12 or 15-foot tree that can be managed much more easily. Full-size apple trees should be planted no closer than 30' apart (nor should other trees be planted closer than that to the apple). Dwarfs can be set 12' apart.

Even peaches, though short-lived, may grow too high to spray and pick easily; dwarf varieties again are more convenient. For peaches and apricots, get the hardiest kind suitable to your area.

As with other food crops, though, don't plant fruit trees unless you are prepared to give them the kind of care they need, and this includes regular spraying for insects and disease virtually from the time that spring buds show green until just before harvest. An unsprayed fruit tree is just a source of infection in the neighborhood.

When grown in sod as most home trees are, an annual spring fertilization is necessary to ensure proper growth and fruit production. Treat as for shade trees (see Chapter 6).

Most fruit trees in good season will set more fruit than they can either support or nurture. In such years there is a heavy June drop of green fruit, which is normal. Many trees, especially apples and crabs, are naturally biennial bearers. Severe thinning of the fruit will not only make the remaining fruit larger, but will influence the tree to bear some the next year when it would not normally.

7-7. Rhododendrons and Acid-Soil Plants

There is a group of plants that requires an acid soil. They are variously called "acid-soil", "ericaceous" or "lime-hating", which isn't strictly true. It is the alkaline condition of the soil they can't get along in. Among them are blueberries, mentioned earlier in the chapter.

It also includes some fine flowering plants such as azaleas and rhododendrons, andromeda, heather and heath, and leucothoe. They are not among the hardiest of garden subjects, but they can be grown successfully north to southern Ontario, the Maritimes and in selected places along the St. Lawrence if their particular soil requirements are met, as well as in south coastal British Columbia and milder areas in the U.S. where they are quite common.

Essentially they need a highly humus soil,

acid in reaction, that will hold summer moisture — they are shallow-rooted — yet is perfectly drained. (Heaths and heathers do best in a soil of granite sand.)

The easiest way to arrange suitable soil conditions for ericacious plants is to make a bed of sphagnum peat moss, or peat moss and gritty sand, that is slightly raised above the surrounding ground. Since they also need shade from the winter winds and sun, and since they get along nicely in part or dappled shade, make the bed on the north or west side of tall evergreens or a building, or under high branched oaks.

Except for heather and heath which prefer a soil on the dry side, provide plenty of moisture over the summer, and make sure the plants go into the winter turgid. Their fertilizer needs are small. Well-rotted or dehydrated manure applied in early spring as a top-dressing, alone or mixed with fresh peat moss, will supply all they need of the major minerals. But yellowing leaves indicate an inability to get iron. You can supply this with micro-fine iron powder sold for the purpose, ferrous (iron) sulphate in water solution, or chelated iron according to package directions. Dusting the soil surface with powdered sulphur till it is yellow annually will help maintain acidity.

Chicago Peace

E.H. Morse

Electron

Arlene Francis

Brasilia

Adolf Horstmann

Roses are not easy to grow because they attract insects and disease, but the beautiful flowers they produce make up for their shortcomings.

Shade Gardening

The irony of growing your garden well, watering, fertilizing and protecting against insects and disease, is that its nature changes. From a young garden with lots of sunlight — too much on those hot summer days — you now find difficulty in growing sun-loving summer flowers, vegetables, fruit.

Or perhaps you've just bought an older house with a jungle of uncared for plants, much shade and no idea of how to go about turning it into a garden.

Perhaps the first step is to decide how you want to deal with it. The most direct way is to clear out all the mature plants, all the tangles of foliage, and start over again. And this may be the wisest choice in an old garden. While it is possible to cut back and revitalize many shrubs and evergreens, it will be years before they look good again. Even so, they may not be the kinds of plants you'd choose anyway.

On the other hand, you may decide you want to live with the shade by changing your garden techniques, giving up growing certain kinds of plants, merely getting rid of some of the worst existing specimens.

Survey the tree shade situation. If there are trees in yards on either side of you, you probably don't need the tree (or trees) on your own property and could have it removed by a professional tree firm. Indeed, if the existing tree shows any signs of ill health, such as dead branches or trunk rot, you will be saving yourself great trouble later by

having it removed now.

Since firewood is so expensive in cities now, make a deal with the tree firm either to cut the price by the amount of firewood recovered, or to cut it up so you can use it.

When it comes time for removal, decide how low or high you want the trunk stub to remain. Cut off at ground surface, the stump is inconspicuous and there is no need to try to excavate the roots which will gradually rot away, albeit nourishing some toadstools over the next few years.

You could cut it at bench height for a garden seat, or pole height to accommodate planters with trailing plants that would drip down and perhaps meet a climber (see vines, Chapter 5) coming up from the ground below.

If you're waffling on a decision about removing an existing tree, checking to see what kind it is may help you come to a conclusion. An oak, for example, is tap-rooted, and doesn't permeate the top six inches of soil so that other plants can't grow. A birch or locust has fine leaves which let through a dappled shade, again allowing other plants to grow underneath. Norway, silver and Manitoba maples either provide dense shade or permeate the ground with roots, or both. Even worse are poplars and willows, which can damage conduits and even foundation walls, and have no place in any small garden. They are also subject to storm damage and may take out utility wires.

8-1. Try High Pruning

If you decide to keep the tree, you can still improve conditions for other plants in your garden by high pruning. This consists in removing all lower branches flush with the trunk; the height to which you remove them will depend on the size of the tree. But such removal won't really hurt the tree — it is only emulating what happens in the forest where shaded lower branches die naturally and drop off, the crown of the tree reaching up for light.

High pruning lets light come in from underneath and allows you to grow more plants, providing the soil is not permeated with roots. This root competition for actual space, minerals and water is as damaging to smaller plants as the actual lack of light.

While there is something you can do about trees in your own yard, there is little to be done about the neighbors' (in most places it is legal to remove any branches that trespass on your property, but if you do, and something happens to the tree, you are responsible). Nor can you do anything about the shade from nearby structures, particularly high-rises.

Just as unsuitable trees should come out, so should overgrown shrubs. There is no way, for example, to prune back an old lilac that dominates a small garden and keep the lilac small. The big old roots will send up suckers as fast as you can cut them out, and the ground around is so permeated with them you can't grow anything else anywhere near. The chances are anyway that nice as lilac flowers are in late spring, the old bush is producing fewer and fewer, and they are higher and higher up.

Do old foundation evergreens have more wood showing than needles, and overlap the path and driveway — and keep light from house windows? Have shrubs grown into each other so you can't tell one from another? Again, the only real remedy is to be brutal and remove them. Use the space for other kinds of plants, or for genuine dwarfs that will stay small, neither taking up so much room again nor shading the area all around them.

Sometimes such a severe thinning — removing three quarters or more of the large plants in your garden plus removal or high pruning of a tree — will accomplish what you want. The competition and shade will be reduced to the point where you can grow flowers, some salad greens and a few perennials, and a lawn that doesn't look as though it's about to expire.

8-2. Soil Needs Attention

Improve the soil you're working with. Remember that in heavy shade it is likely to remain damp a long time after a heavy rain, and stay that way during late fall and early spring. Improving drainage, mixing a good deal of sand into the soil or importing sandy loam to build up the height will help reduce the dampness problem. Be prepared to deal with powdery mildew that thrives in very humid conditions. And don't have the area enclosed entirely with a board fence or a hedge that will prevent air from moving through.

Ironically the same shady garden that is wet in spring and fall and never seems to dry out, does indeed, suddenly, with active growth of the trees as the weather warms up. All those roots in the same plot of ground suck it dry so that watering grass and other plants becomes critical. They may need a soaking daily in hot, dry, windy weather.

Assess the kind of shade you have to deal with. Does the sun come in at all? Do you get a minimum of six hours of direct sunlight a day during summer at least in some part of the garden? That's a critical amount that may allow you to grow more kinds of plants than you thought. Is there a spot that gets sun most of the day or a wall or fence that does? That might be the place to grow roses, or a vegetable garden, or a sun-loving plant trained to a flat surface.

If so, the key to success probably lies in whether the soil itself is free of pervading roots, or whether it is permeated. You can find this out by digging the area with a spade. A pervasive tree or shrub will fill the earth around with woody roots that support clusters of fine, hair roots at intervals. These are the feeder roots that absorb the soil moisture which contains the dissolved minerals necessary for growth.

If the ground is pervaded with them, it may be worth it to you to construct either a retaining wall or an in-ground concrete planter that will thwart the roots and allow you to grow your favorite plants.

And even if you can't grow the same bright summer flowers you're accustomed to, or that your friends are able to grow, there will be something that will succeed. You can make a point of a board, cane or vertical pole fence or masonry walls. A fountain with a recirculating pump, a trickle of water over porous limestone rocks that will support lichens and moss on their surface all summer, a piece of garden statuary, a birdbath combined with an all-year feeder station plus hanging pots and baskets of foliage plants; and house plants out for the summer (African violets bloom well in shady locations) can produce a green garden every bit as interesting, if not as brightly colored, as the traditional ones.

Hydrangea petiolaris (climbing hydrangea) is one of few deciduous shrubs that will grow in dense shade.

8-3. Dealing with Heavy Shade

In very dense shade all day the kind of gardening you can do is very limited. Grass-growing is so unrewarding that you should entirely abandon the idea of a lawn. Instead, use natural paving stone, bricks, decorative large stones, small colored or white stone, wood rounds, logs, chips and bark chips, alone or in combination to cover the ground in patterns and designs.

These could be alternated with plantings of periwinkle *(Vinca minor)* which has glossy green leaves and blue flowers, and stays prostrate. If there isn't enough soil to plant it in, build retainers around the base of trees and fill them with topsoil brought in. The periwinkle will soon cover the surface and from then on a light clipping with grass shears twice a season will keep it in place.

Among evergreens you could try are chamaecyparis, euonymus, Japanese spurge,

Trying to garden in heavy shade may require first buying pots of spring bulbs brought into bud by commercial growers; then replacing these with annual flowers, and finally, replacing the annuals with florist-grown chrysanthemums.

eastern white cedar, dwarf globe cedar, andromeda, leucothoe, mountain laurel and rhododendrons (the latter four in acid soil), Japanese yew and boxwood.

Among deciduous shrubs, the Saskatoon and others of the serviceberry family may succeed; alder, petiolaris hydrangea, St. John's wort, elder and various viburnums.

One of the best ground covers for areas in dense shade is periwinkle (Vinca minor) which has glossy green leaves and blue flowers.

Among vines, try Virginia creeper, euonymus and bittersweet.

For perennial flowers try plantain lily which has a variety with variegated leaves that adds some color, as well as its flowers; lily-of-the-valley, and summer foliage plants.

For summer flowers: garden balsam, collinsia, forget-me-not, foxglove, godetia, impatiens, lobelia, monkey flower, nemophilia, nicotiana, pansy, torenia, Virginia stock — foliage will be good but flowers few. Try coleus and bulbous caladiums for colorful leaves. White flowers generally produce best.

In addition, during the frost-free season, all foliage house plants plus African violets can be brought out to decorate the "green garden". Extra rooted cuttings can be set into the garden soil, or used to interplant with some of the above kinds for mixed summer planters.

Home owners with a heavy shade problem can do as suggested for apartment gardeners in Chapter 4: buy pots of spring bulbs brought into bud by commercial growers for containers. Replace them with annual flowers till they look poorly. Replace again with geraniums in bloom. Finally, replace the now-fading geraniums with florist-grown chrysanthemums.

Hardy spring bulbs may be treated as winter annuals. Plant top-size bulbs in September-October. They have the flower built in and will bloom reliably the next spring, even under heavy shade. Discard them when bloom is over. Treat hardy lilies the same way.

You might even get a bonus with the very early-flowering bulbs. If they grow early enough, and your shade all comes from deciduous trees, enough sun may come through for them to fatten up enough for another year's spring bloom before the leaves come out.

8-4. Dappled Shade

If your shade is dappled and the sun peeps in now and then, you'll be able to grow all the plants named above and probably a great many more, too, including a lawn. Experiment to see what does well, discarding any that grow tall and lank, and produce few or no flowers. Check with your local nurseryman and agricultural experimental station, but some or all of the following flowers should do well:

Anchusa; wax, tuberous and foliage begonias; caladium; calliopsis, calendula; cam-

The purple grape hyacinth here provides a bright border for multi-colored tulips. (Photo by Malak)

Columbine is a short-lived perennial that grows well in dappled shade.

Petunias and ageratum in a spot garden.

panulata, China aster, centaurea, clarkia, cleome, cosmos, cynoglossum, dianthus (pinks); dusty miller, English daisy (short-lived perennial), feverfew, honesty, larkspur, lupine, petunia, phlox drummondi, blue and red salvia, schizanthus, snapdragon, sweet alyssum, verbena.

It should be possible to grow salad greens and perhaps tomatoes in the sunniest spot, or in containers moved to catch the sun.

Creeping red fescue and its modern, improved varieties will succeed better than Kentucky bluegrass and its varieties. An old lawn that began with Kentucky bluegrass could be overseeded with red fescue as described in Chapter 2.

A good deal of the secret of growing grass under unfavorable conditions lies in the maintenance you give it — providing more than the usual amount of fertilizer and water, and spreading worked compost or topsoil

These dianthus Magic Charms won a bronze medal in the 1974 All-America selections.

Very often in such conditions, regular fertilization and watering if the soil is dry result in the grass coming back and the moss vanishing.

8-5. Try Anything on Six Hours' Sun

If your garden, or any part of it, gets six hours or more of direct sun a day, you'll have a much wider choice of what you can grow. It will support any of the flowers and other plants mentioned above and will probably also let you grow the standard summer annuals. There'll be a little more leafy growth and a little less flowering and fruiting, but try roses, perennials, tomatoes, beans, peas, carrots, beets, broccoli (as well as the leafy vegetables).

Peonies, delphinium, iris, phlox (perennial) and 'mums will produce some flowers, especially if given some space to develop.

Choice of shrubs and evergreens will be vastly enlarged too. Six hours' sunlight a day will support most dwarf junipers, specimen junipers, spruce, and dwarf, ball pines (at least in their younger years) as well as the shrubs and evergreens mentioned earlier.

If you have a wall or fence in the full sun consider training a juniper, decorative shrub, or fruit tree to take advantage of the sunlight and the small space, and decorate the surface at the same time. The flowering vine clematis seems a natural for such a situation as it prefers its roots in the shade. A recurrent blooming climbing rose tied to a support provides as good summer flower color as you can find, and cut roses for the house as well.

over the area annually. This helps make up for the root competition.

Many gardeners believe that shade is the only reason for failure with grass. Some blame an acid soil without having the soil tested to see if it is in fact acid (many American and most Canadian soils are alkaline). In fact, the likely culprit is an impoverished soil. Moss often appears after the grass dies out because it can live in much poorer conditions than grass can — moss does not kill the grass.

The flowers in this colorful, well-planned garden repeat the straight lines of the fence and walks. (Photo by Malak)

9 Try Something Unusual

Sometimes a well-planted and well-tended garden seems to require some special plant — an accent, a novelty, something to attract the eye particularly during the whole growing season.

9-1. Trees with Weeping Forms

Weeping types of trees have always had an attraction for people. But the one most commonly planted, weeping willow, is completely unsuitable to all but the largest gardens, and even then should be planted by water in an area not required for any other purpose. They are very big and they continually drop twigs and leaves, to say nothing of branches in storms.

Fortunately there are a number of other trees with weeping forms that suit the small to medium garden, including some very hardy ones, even on the prairies. One of the smallest is the weeping form of the Siberian pea shrub, caragana, long familiar in its upright form as a hedge and windbreak plant in the midwest. Pendula, the weeping form, is a grafted tree on a four-foot stem that never grows any taller, although it does get bigger around as it gets older. Thus it is suitable for even the

Young's weeping birch is hardy and though it grows over 30 feet high, its branches always weep to the ground.

smallest garden with a patch of full sunlight.

It is a legume, will get along in poor soil and a dry location once established, and is extremely cold and wind-hardy. Like its upright cousins, it bears bright yellow, pea-like flowers with a sweet nectar at their base that children like to taste. It should be grown to a stake for the first several years at least.

Also very hardy is the weeping version of the European white birch — Young's weeping birch. It will eventually grow over 30 feet high but always maintains branches that weep to the ground. The branch wood itself starts downward and then recurves up, but bears twigs and branchlets that weep foliage down to the ground in a picturesque way. This tree looks best as a single specimen in the center of a well-kept lawn, or planted in front of darker-foliaged evergreens where its light green foliage stands out in summer, and its (eventually) whitish bark in winter.

There is another form that doesn't weep to the ground, though it has pendulous branches, but its leaves are deeply and finely cut, making them look very light and lacy. European white birch does not have a long lifespan, however, and is subject to both birch leaf miner and the bronze birch borer in some areas.

A weeping tree suited to small gardens but only in milder areas is the purple-leafed beech (*purpureo-pendula*) – a double accent plant. The leaf color is a dull maroon red-to-purple. Branches weep or trail almost to the ground and the tree is very slow-growing so not likely to take over the garden. Maximum height is about 20 feet.

For large properties there is a standard, green-leafed version of the European beech that produces a twisted mass of branches that often hide the trunk completely. Pendula is faster-growing than the purple weeper, and reaches a greater height – 60 feet or more, with a large crown.

Red Jade crabapple, hardy to Ottawa, has branches that weep or trail to the ground, and within a few years of planting these bear small, bright red crabapples which hang on well past fall, accounting for its name. It is a small tree that seldom grows above 18 feet, and takes many years to reach that. Red Jade is an ideal plant to place where it can be seen from a house door or window.

Hardier than Red Jade is the weeping form of the Asiatic mulberry, the tree that feeds silkworms and that has been cultivated for 2,500 years. As with most weeping forms, the desired variety is grafted on seedling roots and stem, so beware of hard pruning the top – if you cut it below the graft it won't weep any more.

Even the central shoot of weeping mulberry grows down. New shoots appear from this to grow up for a while and then down again. It produces a heavy growth that is continually enlarging, but it never becomes a really tall tree. It looks particularly good in a formal garden when surrounded by clipped evergreens or hedges.

Perhaps the most spectacular of all weeping trees in early spring is the weeping form of the Japanese flowering cherry, the Higan weeping cherry.

A moderate-sized tree up to 20 feet, it produces crooked, pendulous branches with pale rose to white single blossoms in masses, a breath-taking sight, especially if the plant is viewed from a distance, ideally with a water background and lots of room to show it off. Since flowers appear before the leaves they are even more conspicuous than some of the larger-flowered non-weeping Japanese cherries. This tree would be a first choice for a Japanese type garden where it is hardy – in areas with mild winters.

Even tenderer, but also spectacular in a different way in late spring, is the Waterer laburnum, a small 20- to 25-foot tree that drips foot-long clusters of golden yellow flowers, although the tree itself does not weep. It is generally listed as hardy in areas with mild winters, but it is subject to damage from the March sun; it should be placed where it gets shelter both from the winter sun and the wind. It needs staking for the first few years.

9-2. Tree Forms of Flowering Shrubs

There are a number of man-made small trees ideal as accent plants in small formal gardens, divisions of larger gardens, or for the brief planting spaces allotted to town houses.

Tree roses are perhaps the most impressive, although they require the most care – in all but the mildest climates they will not survive the winter if left in place, upright.

The trick is to shorten all canes at the top back to six inches, excavate a trench deep

This girl participates in a public school community garden program. She is picking zinnias to take home.

There are, however, other flowering shrubs commonly made into a tree form that are far easier to look after and much hardier. Probably the hardiest is the tree form of the flowering almond (also sometimes called "flowering plum", *Prunus triloba multiplex*). The flowering top is grafted on four-foot stem from which new growth will eventually reach up to 12 or 15 feet maximum. Flowering is the same as for the bush; double, pink flowers cover all the twigs before the leaves appear in spring. Unfortunately the plant is not distinguished during the rest of the season.

The well-known PeeGee hydrangea with its large, white, cone-shaped flowers that turn pink and last into winter, is available grafted on to a four-foot stem that will eventually grow eight to ten feet. Besides being suitable to tiny gardens, the tree hydrangea is valuable because its flowers appear in August when few others do.

Two kinds of lilacs are available in tree form, a distinct advantage not only for the gardener on smaller spaces but also for larger gardens where the suckering of common lilacs is undesirable.

The Japanese tree lilac grows naturally to one or two trunks, eventually getting up to 25 or 30 feet. It has the advantage of blooming two weeks or more after the common lilacs, and so can extend the season. Its flowers are creamy white. In winter the Japanese tree lilac presents a particularly attractive skeleton of fine branchlets, and its deep maroon, cherry-like bark stands out in the winter sunlight.

Several kinds of French hybrid lilacs come grafted on to four-foot stems so that they grow as small trees, making them safe to plant among other shrubs or in the lawn. Both the Japanese lilac and French hybrids are hardy on the prairies.

Just as hardy is the European snowball (*Viburnum opulus*) with a four-foot, grafted stem. Like the shrubby form, it produces its round heads of white flowers in late spring; leaves are bright red in fall. And it will grow in a shady location.

One of the most highly perfumed garden plants is the Carlesi or Korean spice viburnum. One plant will perfume your garden — and your house on a warm day in May when

enough to accommodate the rose, loosen the soil and roots on the opposite side, and tip the tree over horizontally in the trench. Then cover with sufficient earth to protect from winter's cold. Or you could grow it in a large, open-weave plastic clothes basket. In late fall, dig up the basket, cutting off any roots sticking through. Move the tree, basket, soil and all to the back garden and bury it in a trench as with the first method.

There's no disputing how eye-catching tree roses are. The rose flowers are full-size hybrid teas, virtually at eye level. And when the flowers reach full bloom the leaves are almost hidden. But because of the winter care involved, and the fact tree roses need as much care in the growing season as a bush-type hybrid tea, they are really a hobbyist item.

The multi-stemmed Japanese tree lilac blooms two weeks or more after the common lilacs. Its flowers are creamy white.

the windows are open. Normally grown as a shrub in the border, it is also available as a four-foot standard. It has attractive grooved and pebbled foliage, white flowers with a pinkish tinge and delicious, spicy perfume. It will also stand considerable shade. It suits a small garden as it rarely grows over ten feet. It is hardy only in areas with mild winters.

Not a flowering shrub-tree in the usual sense of spectacular blooms, but closest to a broad-leafed evergreen tree outside of south coastal British Columbia and milder areas, is the tree euonymus. This, too, is a manufactured plant, with an evergreen (in mild winters) top grafted on to a four-foot stem, an ultimate spread of five feet and height of about ten feet. The variegated version has silver- or white-edged green leaves. Hardy from the 44th parallel south, it will lose its leaves in a severe winter or where exposed to the March wind or sun. Both make perfect little formal trees suitable for a small or formal garden.

It is essential to provide support for these little trees for several years after transplanting. Tree roses should always be supported by ties to a stake, since they are topheavy. And because roses are dug up each fall they don't get a chance to establish their roots in the soil around to anchor them as other trees (shrubs on standards) do. Otherwise plant them as you would any other small tree, and give them the same after-care.

9-3. Other Dramatic Specimens

Some woody plants attract attention by their pecular habit of growth. One that is often pounced upon by flower arrangers who always seem to have a need for a twisted branch is the corkscrew hazel. It's a medium tall shrub that produces gnarled and whorled branches with turned and interlaced twigs, somewhat like live driftwood. Obviously it is just as interesting, if not more so, in winter without its leaves as it is in summer. Early bloom before the leaves unfold is often nipped by frost so only occasionally, except in the mildest climates, are the edible filberts produced. A non-contorted close relative, *atropurpurea,* has purplish or brownish leaves all season.

Sir Harry Lauder's walking stick is the popular name given to an unusual, heavily thorned aralia that has many seasons of interest. When small and leafless in winter, it resembles a tall, skinny cactus. Its leaves are large and compound, consisting of many leaflets, sometimes three feet long and doubly compound – a very handsome summer dress indeed. In addition, it has large, white flower clusters in August. It stands city conditions and hot, dry locations well, and never grows over 25 feet. Its fruit is black. The Angelica tree, as it is sometimes also called, is hardy only to the 44th parallel and milder areas.

The corkscrew willow not only has twisted and contorted branches and twigs, but also twisted leaves, so that it is a curiosity summer and winter, as well as a source of materials for unusual or oriental flower arrangements. It has olive-green leaves and twigs to match. But unlike the weeping willow and most other tree willows, it is a small tree, never growing over 35 to 40 feet tall even in maturity. It is hardy as far north as the 45th parallel and in the mildest climates may be grown as a tubbed specimen on balconies, patios or roof gardens.

9-4. Trees with Historical Interest

Some trees may be attractive to you because of their historical interest. One is the Dawn redwood, so called because it is older than the North American redwood, dating back to the dawn of history. It was not known that live specimens survived and a Japanese botanist described the plant from fossil remains some 34 years ago. Three years later, a Chinese forest researcher collected live plants, not knowing what they were or that they had been written up in Japan. A year or two later researchers matched them up, assigning the specimens to the name "Metasequoia" ("meta" meaning "before", "sequoia", the Indian name for redwood). A Chinese expedition was sent out to bring back some live specimens, parts of which were sent to Harvard University's Arnold Arboretum where the director decided he wanted some seeds. He made a grant to a Chinese botanist to get them and some arrived in North America in 1948.

These were widely distributed, some going to Ottawa. Another parcel of seeds arrived just before the Communist take-over of China, and these were also distributed, so the oldest Dawn redwood tree outside of China is 27 years old at this writing.

Dawn redwood is available from nurseries as young trees and rooted cuttings and makes a fine plant where you have room. It is a conifer with lacy, fern-like needles, but deciduous like the larches. Just before the leaves fall they turn a bronzy-purple. It is extremely fast-growing, sometimes doubling its height in one summer, and is hardy as far north as the 45th parallel (where it is slower-growing mainly on account of frost killing back some of the central shoot growth).

It has red, exfoliating bark (bark that peels and sheds naturally), and freely puts out new shoots from old wood. It grows well in moist (although not waterlogged) soil, and may grow 100 feet high in good locations. Apparently the wood is not useful for anything but fuel.

Because it has an open branching habit, it looks good grown in groups, but single specimens may be pruned for denser growth.

9-5. The Oldest Living Tree

The bristlecone pine, on the other hand, is a small, extremely slow-growing tree. Very hardy, it is doubtful that it ever grows over 40 feet and probably not half that in most locations. The historical interest here is that bristlecone pines in the U.S. Rockies are thought to be over 4,000 years old, the oldest living trees in the world. In rugged, exposed situations, they have the ability to let one part of the trunk die while other sections keep on growing. Some of the oldest are under 20 feet high, huge around the base, but still clinging to life.

The little plant you get from a nursery makes an ideal conversation piece. Plant it in a rock garden, among miniatures of many kinds of plants, or in an arrangement of rocks and other dwarf evergreens to simulate mountain landscapes. In garden culture, at least at first, bristlecone tends to grow about as broad as it does high. Needles, in bunches of five, are from one to five inches long, and appear silvery or white from the resin that covers them. Nursery plants will be only a few inches high.

9-6. Living Fossil Tree

Much more commonly planted though still rare enough to be noted is the ginkgo or maidenhair tree. There are few natural or wild ginkgos left in the world, and indeed it is often called a "living fossil tree". It is the only remaining species of its family, many of which once thrived hundreds of millions of years ago. The ginkgo is related to the conifers yet has some characteristics of broad-leafed trees. Its leaves, for example, are broad and flat, but with fan-shaped veins somewhat resembling the maidenhair fern.

Ginkgo trees bear flowers when mature, but there are separate male and female trees. The method of flower bearing is the same as for conifers but the seed, instead of falling free from the scales of a cone, develops a fleshy covering that looks like fruit. These make a mess, and have an objectionable smell, so nurseries propagate only male trees by root cuttings.

At first, young ginkgos grow narrowly upright, but as they mature they develop a rounded head. They are slow-growing, resistant to city smog, apparently free of both pests and disease, and live to a great old age. Ginkgo is hardy to the 45th parallel and makes a fine street tree.

The ginkgo we plant is descended from temple trees from China or Japan where it was brought many hundreds of years ago. There the seeds were roasted and eaten, and the trees themselves were believed to be able to turn back fire. (A temple planted with ginkgos was saved from fire after the 1923 Tokyo earthquake.)

9-7. Fit for a King

Most gardeners are familiar with the herbaceous peony that dies to the ground each fall. There is another woody, shrub peony, for some unknown reason called "tree peony", that maintains woody stems above ground all season, as does any other shrub. It produces

Generous plantings of hybrid teas, floribundas and grandifloras can be used as a divider or screen separating lawn from driveway.

even more spectacular, larger and earlier flowers than the herbaceous form, and in colors unavailable in peonies otherwise, including yellow and purple.

In fact, bloom is so spectacular that Chinese emperors decreed it to be for royal gardens only, and it is said you could lose your head for having a tree peony elsewhere. It was grown in its natural shrubby form and as an espalier trained to walls.

Monks took the tree peony to Japan some 1,200 to 1,600 years ago where it was cultivated and planted in show gardens particularly for women. Varieties available to us are variously from China through Europe, from Japan or from hybrids developed in various parts of the world. Here they are generally sold by color of the flower, but singles, semi-doubles and doubles are available.

The most inexpensive plants are available as new grafts, with the tree peony tops growing on herbaceous peony roots, since

the latter are more vigorous, at least at first. Thus the little plant must be set deep enough in the ground so the top graft will develop its own roots, and the grafted roots discouraged from sending up tops (see Chapter 1). Allow several years for the plants to become established before you expect flowers. Then you'll get an ever increasing number each succeeding year. It is essential that plants have shelter from the wind. They can be interplanted with other shrubs and evergreens, used alone as a single specimen or planted together in different colors. They are rated hardy only in areas with mild winters, although gardeners from the prairies have been known to order them (perhaps heavy winter covering will keep them alive).

Planting is usually recommended in October, although early spring planting as soon as the ground is workable is satisfactory. The soil should be worked well, be enriched and alkaline. Good drainage is necessary.

Collections of tree peonies can be seen in

bloom in May at the Royal Botanical Gardens, Hamilton, the parks in Rochester, New York, and at Swarthmore College in Pennsylvania. Blooming time is a week to two weeks ahead of herbaceous peonies.

9-8. Silver in the Garden

When white appears on a green leaf, it shows up as silver in the garden. It is both cool-looking and bright, in effect adding another color and season-long interest. It doesn't upstage other plants as purple and red-leafed ones do, and it doesn't look as though the leaf is undernourished or dying, as yellow-leafed plants tend to.

In addition, many plants with silver on their leaves have other qualities as well, such as flowers, colored fruit or twigs, that make them valuable alone or in mixed plantings.

One of the hardiest and most satisfactory as a specimen is the silver-leafed dogwood shrub. The basic leaf color is mid to dark green and the white of their edges is very close to a pure white. Hardy on the prairies and quite inexpensive, it deserves wider planting. Ultimate height is six to eight feet, but pruning can keep it in check. Since the best white occurs on new leaves, pruning out old canes encourages new shoots from the roots with brighter white edges. Besides attractive leaves, the plant has white flowers in two-inch clusters in spring. In winter its red twigs are especially notable. It loses attractiveness only in droughts when the white edges turn brownish, so provide extra moisture over the summer.

As a single-stemmed small tree, or a multi-stemmed tall shrub, the Russian olive has gray-green leaves that appear to be silver at a distance, especially when there is a background of shrubs with more typically green leaves. The undersides of the olive's leaves are markedly silvery and even the flowers appear to be silvered. It produces edible yellow fruit from fragrant, greenish flowers.

Another very hardy plant, a native of the prairies, is the buffaloberry. It has leaves with

The white edges on the leaves of the silver-leafed dogwood are very close to pure white. Besides attractive leaves, the plant has white flowers in spring.

a silvery appearance on both sides and red berries in August-September that make a tart jelly. Flowers are yellowish, appearing in late spring. It, too, may be grown as a shrub or as a small tree if kept to one stem.

Much tenderer is Emerald Gaiety euonymus, with white edging to its deep green, leathery leaves. The latter are evergreen in mild winters and especially under snow cover, but like other evergreen euonymuses, it produces a new set each spring anyway. This plant needs regular pruning to remove long, stray shoots, and it may be kept mound-like or be trimmed to a pyramid. It tends to crowd itself if left unpruned.

Silver kerria is hardy as far north as the 45th parallel and more suitable to small gardens, seldom growing three feet tall. It has single white flowers in spring, and an overall silver appearance from its light green leaves edged in white — cut out any shoots, twigs or branches that bear all-green leaves.

A number of evergreens have a silvery look to their green or bluish foliage, particularly in winter. Among them are Hoopsi blue spruce and cultivated varieties of juniper, including both Chinese and western kinds. Blue Haven, very hardy, is an example of the latter, silver pfitzer is a medium-tall shrubby form of

Chinese juniper; mountbatten a silvery upright form.

9-9. Some for the Birds

Almost all plants, small and large, deciduous and evergreen, are valued by the birds as perching and nesting areas, shelter and protection against the weather. But there are some that are especially valuable to them. For example, cedar, spruce, pine and hemlock are all important as winter shelter to our permanent birds, but cedar and hemlock also provide seeds for winter food.

The Russian olive mentioned above produces mealy berries that attract songbirds, mallards, bobwhites, pheasants, ruffled grouse, deer and rabbits, if the raccoons don't clear them off before the snow flies.

The common hackberry tree's greenish-orange fruit is reported to attract 40 species of birds including bluebirds, cardinals, catbirds, grosbeaks, mockingbirds, phoebes, quails, robins, solitaires, fox sparrows, thrashers, titmice, towhees, cedar waxwings and woodpeckers. Hackberry is a tough tree and will grow in city conditions as well as in poor soils. Gardeners in colder areas might consider the lowly Manitoba maple as a substitute, although it is insect-prone and drops it leaves early. It's a prolific seeder and attracts chickadees, purple finches, goldfinches, grosbeaks and nuthatches.

The native high bush cranberry is valued for its red fruit by both wildlife and humans (who can make from it a fine jelly to eat with fowl). The red osier dogwood, a very hardy shrub that will grow in wet locations, provides food and shelter for bluebirds, cardinals, grosbeaks, kingbirds, tanagers, vireos, warblers, cedar waxwings, woodpeckers, partridges and grouse.

Other plants good for the birds include mountain ash, partridgeberry, (a ground creeper on poor, acid soil), all fruit-bearing members of the cherry family including the wild pin-cherry (often called "bird-cherry" for obvious reasons), wild grapes, bittersweet, native hollies, most crabapples, arrowwood and coralberry.

Red flower color is particularly attractive to hummingbirds and they'll migrate to gardens with this color predominating among flowers that yield a lot of nectar. Kinds that they like include common honeysuckle, butterflybush, caragana, hawthorn, coral bells, morning glory, delphinium, sweet william, canna lily and gladiolus.

Of course by planting one, a number, or all the kinds named, you won't immediately have any or all the birds mentioned show up at your garden. It sometimes takes quite a while for the word to pass. But gradually birds that do frequent your part of the country will take advantage of what your garden offers, particularly when food supplies are tight elsewhere.

For example, one spring the robins arrived at our garden before spring did — there were no earthworms available. One chap kept himself going on the seeds from crabapples still on the tree from the previous year. He's been coming back to our garden ever since.

10

Summer Garden Calendar: March to December

10-1. March

Bright sunny days raise hopes the new season will soon arrive — alternating with depressing blasts of winter. But the strengthening sun and lengthening days signal the time to start fertilizing house plants once more. This is also the time to repot them into a container one size larger if they're presently potbound with roots coming through the drainage holes in the bottom. Water whenever the soil surface becomes dry, which should occur more frequently as growth accelerates.

Start tubers of begonias and caladiums into growth indoors under fluorescent lights or in east window sills. You can also sow seeds of long-season annuals, biennials and perennials and Spanish onions indoors if you have good growing conditions: bright light, cool temperatures about 65° by day and 5° to 10° lower by night. Plants to start now are coleus, petunias, pansies, phlox, lobelias, dusty millers, foxgloves, perennial delphiniums and geraniums from seed. The latter take five months before they bloom.

You can also root cuttings of geraniums and impatiens that you've carried over the winter indoors. Geraniums root best in gritty sand watered frequently from the bottom.

From February on, branches of flowering shrubs outdoors can be cut and brought in to a cool room and put in a bucket of water to

Coleus is grown for its decorative, long-lasting foliage.

force into bloom. Pots of bulbs sunk in the garden may also be brought into a cool window sill or under lights to bloom indoors.

Make the first fertilizer application on the lawn (even if it's frozen) some time between St. Patrick's Day and the end of the month. As long as your lawn isn't on a steep slope, you can scatter the fertilizer on top of snow.

If the weather is mild and above 40°, do remedial pruning to repair storm damage, cutting lower branches from trees so you can use the space under them. Exceptions are bleeder trees like maples and birch which are best pruned in late June.

This is an excellent time to prune hedges. Deciduous ones naturally are bare so the whole framework can be seen. Make the cuts at least two inches below where you want the foliage to be.

10-2. April

The time most home gardeners should start seedling plants indoors depends on how good the growing conditions are (see above). If quite good, start a number by the first of the month. If moderately good, wait a week or two so that while the plants do get a head start, they don't spend too much time indoors before being set out in late May.

The first ones you plant indoors in pots or boxes should be the ones that require the longest growing time before maturing. As well as Spanish onions and the flowers mentioned above, these include tomatoes, peppers, eggplant, celery, onions, cauliflower, garden pinks, carnations, portulaca, hollyhock, stocks.

As soon as you can get a spade into the ground is the time to plant (or transplant) all hardy, woody plants: shade and fruit trees, flowering shrubs, evergreens of all sorts, and roses. Use a planting mixture, particularly if your soil is heavy clay or light sand. A transplanting solution will help the plant catch, and will supply all the fertilizer it needs for the first season.

If outdoor conditions are suitable, plant seeds of sweet peas, cornflowers, sweet alyssum, and Iceland poppies. Frost won't hurt them.

Lawns should be raked not only to remove debris, but also accumulated clippings and dead plants that haven't rotted. Place the organic matter on the compost pile. Mow as soon as the grass blades grow over two inches.

Dig vegetable gardens and annual flower beds as the weather indicates. Work organic

Prize-winning petunias edged with alyssum.

matter into both. Prune grapes, clematis, wisteria.

Do not prune spring-flowering shrubs until after they flower or you'll sacrifice the spring display.

Fertilize bulb beds, roses and perennials with a general garden fertilizer, a potato-tomato fertilizer or a bulb mixture. Fertilize deciduous trees with a lawn fertilizer (make more application to the grass where trees or shrubs are growing in sod).

Start fast-growing flowers and vegetables from seed indoors in containers from the middle of the month on. These include cabbage, head lettuce, marigolds, zinnias, morning glories. Cucumbers, melons and squash can be started indoors too, but they should be planted in separate pots so their roots won't be disturbed when set outside.

If you have window sill space, you can also start roots of canna lilies and dahlias in pots for a head start. Gladiolus corms with long shoots can be treated the same way.

10-3. May

The first of the month is the earliest possible

Tulip biflora is among the first flowers to bloom in spring. (Photo by Malak)

time to start even frost hardy vegetables outdoors, and then only in a suitable year. Even where there is no danger of frost, the ground is usually too cold and/or wet, which can rot the seed, so judge by the season. Hardiest vegetables are smooth-seeded peas, beets, radishes, carrots, bunching onions and onion sets. Corn is moderately hardy, often coming again from the roots if nipped by frost. Potatoes are safe if planted in warm ground; a frost won't hurt until the tops have grown.

If the season warrants, set out some boxed plants in flower by the middle of the month.

Plant hardy, woody stock so long as there is no sign of growth. Plants moved after new growth appears should have a ball of earth around them.

Disbud peonies for large bloom. Arrange support for the flowers.

Begin a regular spraying schedule for fruit trees and roses as soon as the first green appears on the leaf buds.

Transplant all seedlings outdoors from May 24 on except heat-lovers like melons and squash, and tuberous begonias, caladiums, dahlias and canna lilies. The latter will do better after June 1, in most areas.

Plant out vegetable and annual flower seed.

Sow vegetables successively so they don't all ripen at the same time.

Glads, too, can be planted successively. They are quite hardy and the first planting can often be made near the beginning of the month. Spray with systemic insecticide as soon as green growth is visible above the soil.

Luxury lawns should get a second application of fertilizer around the middle of the month. This is usually also a good time to apply a combination herbicide if weeds are a problem, or a pre-emergent killer for crabgrass. Grass is usually growing at a fast rate and may need cutting twice a week so you don't take off too much at once.

10-4. June

As indicated, most of the tender summer bulbs and warm weather vegetables, including eggplant, peppers, and tomatoes, do

Warm weather vegetables such as eggplant do better if planted in June rather than May.

better if planted in June rather than in May.

Weeding is a major project this month. Hand cut them below the crown so they won't sprout again or spot spray them with a combination herbicide material.

Prune bleeder-type trees. Water all new transplants as needed. If rains fail give the lawn an inch of water a week and mow frequently.

Maintain spray schedules for susceptible plants.

Continue to plant more vegetables such as extra rows of corn, beans, green onions, radishes, and more gladiolus corms.

Let spring bulb foliage turn brown naturally. Plant annuals between. Water bulbs if there's a drought.

Pinch off between one and two thirds of the new growth on the center shoot of pines and spruces to make them grow denser. Dwarf mugho pines should be sheared. Clip hedges toward the end of the month when new shoots have elongated.

Disbud roses to get better-sized blossoms. This means removing as soon as they are clearly visible all but the end buds of any one flowering shoot. Cut blossoms' stems just above a five-leaflet leaf that points out from the center of the bush. Fertilize and water as necessary. Keep up a regular spraying.

Prune out the oldest wood of spring-flowering shrubs after bloom has faded.

Tie tomatoes, dahlias, peppers, clematis at regular intervals as they grow. Renew ties as needed on young trees and fruit trees on stakes.

Gradually move house plants outside for the summer, giving them an appropriate spot – sun for the sun-lovers, shade for those that need it. Check all plants in containers daily for dryness.

Pinch back tall-growing 'mums to produce branching and more flowers in fall.

Plant some extra annual flower seeds for replacement plants and for containers.

Prepare the garden for holidays by catching up on all weeding and watering and arrange for someone to cut the lawn while you're away.

Toward the end of the month give the lawn the last fertilizer before September.

10-5. July

Grass needs faithfully regular and deep watering if it is to stay green over the summer. Cut once a week even if growth is slow. Cut out weeds as they appear. Repeat spraying may be necessary for some stubborn kinds.

Water the vegetable garden as needed to keep plants growing without setback. Tomatoes particularly should have a regular and even supply of moisture to avoid blossom-end rot on the fruit.

Make a regular check on all plants including trees and shrubs for signs of insect infestation. Spray only when necessary.

Divide and replant overgrown iris plants after bloom fades. Cut back water and fertilize delphiniums for a second blooming in fall.

Extra beans, radishes, carrots, beets, green onions can be planted this month if you have irrigation at hand. They'll produce a new crop in September (except radishes which mature in just over three weeks).

Toward the end of the month, or just before you go on vacation, shear back, fertilize and water shaggy, sprawling petunias to bring on fresh growth and bloom in a few weeks.

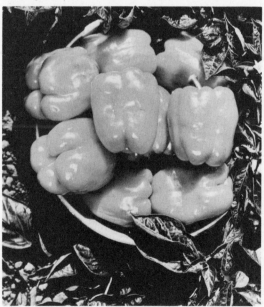

Like eggplant, sweet peppers produce more if planted two or three weeks later than other vegetables.

Remove browned daffodil and tulip foliage by cutting it off with grass shears. Pulling out the old foliage leaves a hole down to the bulb.

Fertilize and water tender summer bulbs, container plants, and vegetables.

Start perennials and biennials from seed outdoors.

Cut back golden mock orange to bring on new shoots with yellow leaves.

As the weather gets warm and muggy, in humid climates powdery mildew will appear. Spray or dust with sulphur susceptible plants such as dahlias, roses, veronica, perennial phlox, perennial asters, tuberous begonias, container plants.

Prune tomatoes for earlier fruit by removing all shoots that appear between the leaf stalk and the main trunk.

10-6. August

Don't fertilize roses after the first of the month, but water all the garden regularly if rains fail. Wash down evergreens with the full force of the hose to clean foliage and drive off red spider mites.

Black-eyed Susans add bright color when planted in mass plantings.

Make the last pinch on 'mums.

Keep pulling lawn weeds including crabgrass to prevent its seeding.

Hoe the vegetable garden regularly or use a mulch to defeat weeds.

Old raspberry canes that have borne fruit should be cut back to the ground.

Plant madonna lily bulbs as soon as available for next year's bloom. Plant fall-blooming crocuses and colchicums for bloom in autumn.

Toward the end of the month, prepare any area you want to seed to grass. Order evergreens for planting at the end of the month. Order hardy spring bulbs for planting in autumn.

Transplant oriental poppies which are virtually dormant now.

Take cuttings of geraniums, impatiens, wax begonias to root for young plants to have indoors over the winter. This is the best way to carry garden geraniums over the winter.

Seeds of salad greens can still be sown in mildest areas.

Repair summer storm damage as soon as you can after it happens.

Keep perennial phlox from going to seed — self-seedlings revert to poor colors.

Maintain sprays on roses, fruit trees, gladiolus, and iris plants against iris borers.

Use spare annual plants to fill in for casualties. Toward the end of the month garden 'mums can be potted for container display.

10-7. September

From the first of the month make new lawns by sowing grass seed on prepared ground.

Feed established lawns and apply herbicide as necessary. Continue to water if rains aren't sufficient. Mow as often as necessary.

Plant evergreens, which are virtually dormant this month.

Touch up prune hedges.

Transplant seedling perennials and biennials.

Move or buy 'mums in bloom for display.

Protect tender summer plants against frost

In September, chrysanthemums may be moved or potted for container display.

to take advantage of possible warmer weather to follow — an old coat works for a few plants.

Move house plants back indoors a few at a time before the furnace runs frequently to get them used to dryer air gradually.

Plant daffodils as soon as available in colder zones, from the middle of the month in longer-season areas. Also plant the little or minor bulbs.

Order deciduous trees and shrubs for planting in October.

If moles, porcupines or other animals dig holes in your lawn the chances are they are looking for grubs that feed on the grass roots. Apply chlordane according to label directions to get rid of the grubs and the animals will dig elsewhere. (Chlordane should be used only once in four years, or less.)

Keep pulling weeds — there is often a fresh crop this month and little ones you missed before are suddenly big. Prevent seeding now and you save work next year.

Collect leaves as they fall so they don't accumulate and smother the grass. Compost them in a separate pile, salting them with earth and lawn fertilizer. Leaf mold is richer, pound for pound, than rotted barn manure.

Bring in a few dwarf annuals to enjoy them for a month or more indoors. Potted tuberous begonias should also be brought in to grow as long as possible.

10-8. October

When you cut down vegetables or frost-killed annuals, leave the roots in place to hold the soil over winter. The tops can go into the compost pile.

Plant garden tulips from the first of the month in short-season areas, from the middle in milder areas.

Plant and transplant deciduous trees and shrubs after the first frost or when the leaves change color, whichever comes first.

Plant peonies, in a well-prepared area in full sun.

Harvest tender bulbs after frost blackens the foliage. Light green tomatoes will ripen indoors. Dark green ones won't.

Luxury lawns get the last fertilizer application of the season late in October.

Tie the branches of upright-type evergreens such as Skyrocket with green garden twine to prevent winter damage.

House plants in window sills need only caretaker service now — with the short dull days of late fall and winter they grow very slowly if at all and need less water and no fertilizer. Plants under fluorescent lights left

Luxury lawns should get their last fertilizer application of the season in late October.

on 16 hours a day should be fertilized and watered normally.

Lay in a supply of hyacinths and paper-whites to force into bloom indoors. Start the first paperwhites in bowls of water and stone chips after the third week of the month.

Break the tops of perennial asters and chrysanthemums over after a heavy frost and leave them that way for winter protection.

Check evergreens to see they go into freeze-up with plenty of moisture in the soil.

10-9. November

Have plenty of topsoil on hand to hill up roses just before freeze-up.

Plant lily bulbs as they are delivered — holes prepared ahead of time can overcome frozen ground.

Extra tulips and daffodils in pots will supply containers in spring if you bury them in sand in the vegetable garden.

Burlap on stakes to shade tender plants from the winter sun will help prevent burning of the foliage. A similar fence can protect against salt-spray from roadways. Protect

evergreens with snow sheds. But don't wrap plants in plastic.

Check stakes and ties to see they are secure for the winter.

Use wire mesh below the snowline to prevent rodent damage to fruit, poplar or birch trees.

Put away summer garden tools after cleaning and oiling them.

If you dig vegetable and flower gardens in fall, simply turn the clods over — let frost do the breaking up.

Increase humidity around house plants with a humidifier or boiling kettle, by growing them in groups on pebble-filled trays in which you keep water just below the pot bottoms, and by syringing leaves daily.

Start amaryllis into growth.

A little extra light, such as from a fluorescent desk lamp, from dusk to bedtime will perk up a tired house plant. The tube should be six inches above the top leaf.

Install bird feeders before freeze-up.

10-10. December

Don't use salt to melt ice on steps and walks where it can get on plants. Instead use

Holes for lily bulbs can be prepared ahead of time to solve the problem of frozen ground. (Photo by Malak)

Bridal Crown is an ivory-white double-flowered daffodil with orange centers to the flowers. (Photo by Malak)

ammonium nitrate or urea. Avoid shovelling snow on to dwarf evergreens; snow can break them down.

Break ice from overweighted tree branches with a pole or piece of lumber after an ice storm. If the weather is mild you can use water from the garden hose to melt it.

Check to see there is surface drainage from winter rains — water should not stand around plants.

When stringing lights for Christmas decora-tions, make sure the bulbs point away from the foliage or bark so the heat won't damage them. Use miniature lights on small trees in pots for steps, patios and apartment balco-nies.

Bulbs that will bloom by Christmas: amaryl-lis, paperwhites, soleil d'or, early hyacinths.

Give gardeners on your list books on the subject, nursery gift certificates, live plants.

Keep water in the cup under the Christmas tree.

Appendix

TULIP GROWTH CYCLE

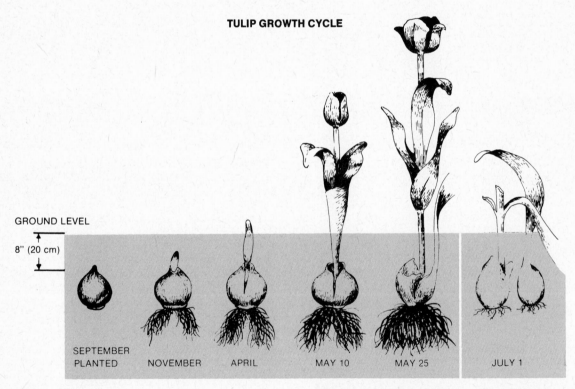

GROUND LEVEL

8" (20 cm)

SEPTEMBER PLANTED | NOVEMBER | APRIL | MAY 10 | MAY 25 | JULY 1

Chart from "Flowering Bulbs for Canadian Gardens", courtesy of Agriculture Canada

TYPES OF BULBS

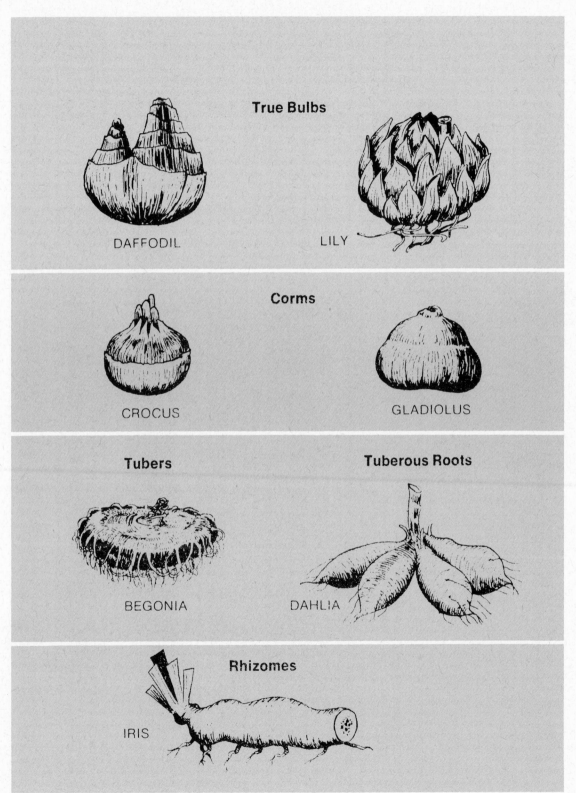

Chart from "Flowering Bulbs for Canadian Gardens",
courtesy of Agriculture Canada

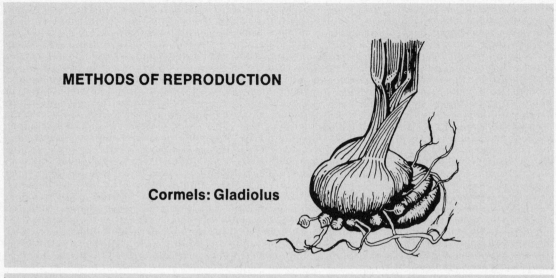

METHODS OF REPRODUCTION

Cormels: Gladiolus

Division: Daffodil

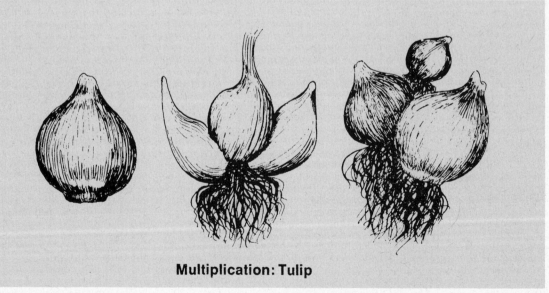

Multiplication: Tulip

Chart from "Flowering Bulbs for Canadian Gardens",
courtesy of Agriculture Canada

METRIC EQUIVALENTS

LENGTH

inch	= 2.54 cm	millimetre	= 0.039 in.
foot	= 0.3048 m	centimetre	= 0.394 in.
yard	= 0.914 m	decimetre	= 3.937 in.
mile	= 1.609 km	metre	= 3.28 ft
		kilometre	= 0.621 mile

AREA

square inch	= 6.452 cm²	cm²	= 0.155 sq in.
square foot	= 0.093 m²	m²	= 1.196 sq yd
square yard	= 0.836 m²	km²	= 0.386 sq mile
square mile	= 2.59 km²	ha	= 2.471 ac
acre	= 0.405 ha		

VOLUME (DRY)

cubic inch	= 16.387 cm³	cm³	= 0.061 cu in.
cubic foot	= 0.028 m³	m³	= 31.338 cu ft
cubic yard	= 0.765 m³	hectolitre	= 2.8 bu
bushel	= 36.368 litres	m³	= 1.308 cu yd
board foot	= 0.0024 m³		

VOLUME (LIQUID)

fluid ounce (Imp)	= 28.412 ml	litre	= 35.2 fluid oz
pint	= 0.568 litre	hectolitre	= 26.418 gal
gallon	= 4.546 litres		

WEIGHT

ounce	= 28.349 g	gram	= 0.035 oz avdp
pound	= 453.592 g	kilogram	= 2.205 lb avdp
hundredweight (Imp)	= 45.359 kg	tonne	= 1.102 short ton
ton	= 0.907 tonne		

PROPORTION

1 gal/acre	= 11.232 litres/ha	1 litre/ha	= 14.24 fluid oz/acre
1 lb/acre	= 1.120 kg/ha	1 kg/ha	= 14.5 oz avdp/acre
1 lb/sq in.	= 0.0702 kg/cm²	1 kg/cm²	= 14.227 lb/sq in.
1 bu/acre	= 0.898 hl/ha	1 hl/ha	= 1.112 bu/acre

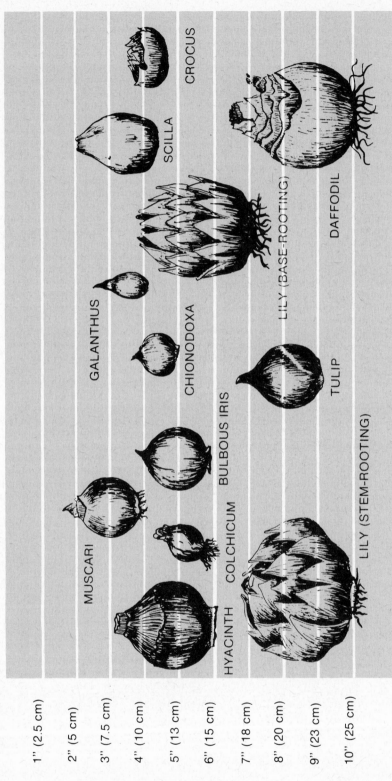

PLANT IN FALL

GROUND LEVEL

1'' (2.5 cm)

2'' (5 cm)

3'' (7.5 cm)

4'' (10 cm)

5'' (13 cm)

6'' (15 cm)

7'' (18 cm)

8'' (20 cm)

9'' (23 cm)

10'' (25 cm)

CROCUS

SCILLA

GALANTHUS

CHIONODOXA

LILY (BASE-ROOTING)

DAFFODIL

BULBOUS IRIS

TULIP

MUSCARI

COLCHICUM

HYACINTH

LILY (STEM-ROOTING)

Chart from ''Flowering Bulbs for Canadian Gardens'', courtesy of Agriculture Canada

PLANT IN SPRING

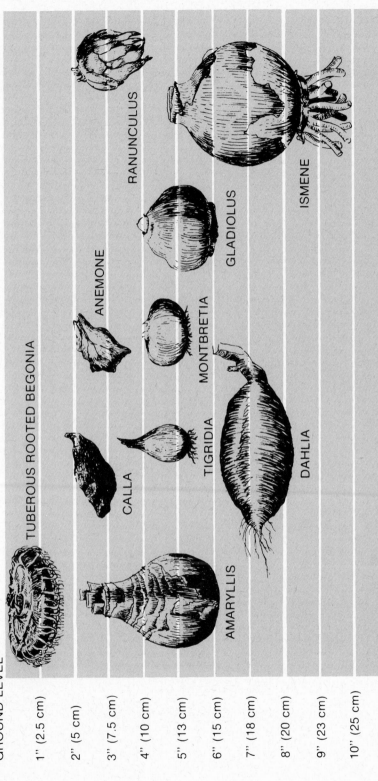

GROUND LEVEL

1" (2.5 cm)

2" (5 cm)

3" (7.5 cm)

4" (10 cm)

5" (13 cm)

6" (15 cm)

7" (18 cm)

8" (20 cm)

9" (23 cm)

10" (25 cm)

TUBEROUS ROOTED BEGONIA

ANEMONE

RANUNCULUS

CALLA

MONTBRETIA

GLADIOLUS

ISMENE

TIGRIDIA

DAHLIA

AMARYLLIS

Chart from "Flowering Bulbs for Canadian Gardens",
courtesy of Agriculture Canada

VEGETABLES FOR APARTMENT GARDENING

Variety	Container & Size	Fertilizer	Number of Plants
Sprite Bush Green Bean	Balcony Planter Box	One handful	Four plants.
Bush Ramano Bean Honey Gold Bush Wax Bean Blue Lake Bush Bean	-------------------------------- 25 inches long by 8 inches wide by 6½ inches deep	Magamp slow release fert- ilizer (7-40-6)	Repeat sowing for continuous crops.
Spring Red Beets	Same As Above	Same As Above	Two rows, 12 plants
Baby Finger Nantes Carrots	Same As Above	Same As Above	Two rows. Thin to 3 inches apart. Sow thinly. Resow after harvest.
Champion Radish Cherry Belle Radish	Same As Above	Same As Above	Sow every two weeks for continuous supply. Don't crowd.
Buttercrunch Lettuce	Same As Above	Two handfuls Magamp slow re- lease fertili- zer (7-40-6)	Six plants. Resow after harvesting each plant.
Ebenezer Onion White Onion	Same As Above	Same As Above	In sets, plant more as onions are harvest- ed. Two rows. Onion seed must be started very early.

Variety	Container & Size	Fertilizer	Number of Plants
Green Curled Endive Full Heart Batavian Escarole	Same As Above	Same As Above	Two plants. Pick leaves for salads or harvest entire plant when mature.
Darki Parsley	Same As Above	Same As Above	Two rows with plants 3 inches apart.
Marjoram Thyme Summer Savory	Same As Above	Same As Above	One row of 6 plants 3 inches apart.
Baron Shumacher S Strawberry	Same As Above	Same As Above	Thin to 8 plants.
Tiny Tim Dwarf Tomato	Same As Above	Same As Above	Thin to 3 plants.
Stakeless Dwarf Tomato	Large Shrub Pot. 10½ inches wide by 9 inches deep	Same As Above	One Plant.
Victory Slicing Cucumber Patio Pick Cucumber	Same As Above	Same As Above	Three plants teepee staked in pot. Use Blossom Set for pollination if bees are not in evidence.

The soil mixture should be 2/3 commercial soil mix, plus 1/3 sand. A medium sized bag (6 lbs.) plus a shovel full of sand will fill the planter box. Slightly more will be needed for the large pot. Do not use BLOSSOM SET on any plants except the Cucumbers and Tomatoes as none of the others requires bees for pollination.

QUICK FACTS ABOUT COMMON ANNUALS

The following table gives at a glance information about common annuals, including how high they grow, common use, the time the seed takes to germinate, how far apart to plant them, and other comments.

PLANT	HEIGHT (Inches)	USES	GERM. (DAYS)	SPAC-ING	NOTES
Ageratum	6-20	Edging.	5	5-10	Cut off dead flowers.
Balsam	12-18	Beds, pots, mixed garden.	10	12-14	Dislikes cold, wet; very frost-sensitive.
Calendula	14-18	Cut flowers, window garden.	10	10-14	Good in cool weather.
Celosia	16-49	Cut flowers, drying.	10	10-20	Needs rich soil.
Coreopsis	18-24	Bedding, edging.	8	10-14	Fast to flower.
Cosmos	30-48	Screen, bedding.	5	12-24	Early types best; pinch back spindly seedlings; thrive in any soil.
Gaillardia	10-20	Cut flowers, drying.	20	10-20	Doubles best.
Marigold	6-30	Bedding, cut flowers, window garden.	5	6-24	Rich soil delays blooming.
Morning glory	8-12 feet	Vine, screen.	5	24-36	Nick seeds to speed germination, sow only when soil warm.
Nasturtium	12	Bedding, edging, boxes.	8	9-12	Blooms in month from seed; needs good drainage, low fertility.
Poppy	12-16	Borders, cut flowers.	10	6-12	Hard to transplant; sow successively.
Portulaca	6-9	Bedding, edging, to hang over low walls.	10	10-12	Loves hot, dry spots; self-sows.
Scabiosa	18-36	Borders, cut flowers.	10	6-12	Needs rich, well-drained soil; cut off old flowers.
Snapdragon	6-36	Beds, borders, cutting.	15	6-24	Fine seed; pinch.
Stocks	24-39	Cut flowers, dwarfs for bedding.	5	10-12	Very fragrant, needs cool weather to flower well.
Sunflower	3-7 feet	Cut flowers, screen, seed, attract birds.	5	12-36	Use new dwarfs for any but largest garden.
Sweet pea	12-48	Cut flowers, screen.	15	8-10	Sow seeds early, need cool weather, rich soil.
Zinnia	6-36	Beds, borders, cut flowers, dwarfs for edging.	5	6-24	Thin after first bloom, removing poor-flowering plants; takes heat well but mildews in high humidity.

GUIDE TO VEGETABLE SEED PLANTING

VARIETY	INDOOR STARTS		OUTDOORS STARTS	BEST SPROUTING TEMP. (°F)	AVG. DAYS TO SPROUT	SEEDING DEPTH/ DIST.	PLANT SPACING
	NECESSARY?	WHEN? (Wk. to last frost)	BEST TIME				
Asparagus	No	—	Late spring through late summer	65° - 75°	14 - 21	½'' deep, 1'' apart	2' after 1st yr.
Beans, Pole	No	—	Early summer through midsummer	70° - 80°	7 - 14	1'' deep, 3'' apart	Hills-3'
Beans, Bush	No	—	Early summer through midsummer	70° - 80°	7 - 14	1'' deep, 3'' apart	6''
Beans, Bush Lima	No	—	Early summer	70° - 80°	14 - 21	1'' deep, 6-8'' apart	12''
Beets & Swiss Chard	No	—	Early summer through late summer	65° - 75°	14 - 21	¼'' deep, 1'' apart	Beets-3'' Sw.Chd-18''
Broccoli & Brussels Sprouts	For spring crop	6 to 8	Late summer for fall crop	65° - 75°	7 - 14	¼'' deep, ¼-½'' apart	1½' 3'
Cabbage & Cauliflower	For spring crop	6 to 8	Late summer for fall crop	65° - 75°	7 - 14	¼'' deep, 1'' apart	Cab.-2' Caul. 2½-3'
Carrots	No	—	Late spring through late summer	65° - 75°	14 - 21	¼'' deep, 1'' apart	1½-2''
Celery	For spring crop	12 to 16	Late summer for fall crop	60° - 70°	14 - 21	1/8'' deep, 1'' apart	6''
Collards	No	—	Early spring where summers are cool late summer elsewhere	65° - 75°	7 - 14	½'' deep, 2'' apart	3' apart
Corn, Sweet	No	—	Early summer through midsummer	65° - 75°	7 - 14	½'' deep, 3'' apart	Hills-3' Rows-12''
Cucumbers	Only short summers	4 to 6	Early summer through midsummer	70° - 80°	7 - 14	1'' deep, 4'' apart	Groups — 4'
Eggplant	Necessary	8 to 12	—	70° - 80°	14 - 21	¼'' deep, ½'' apart	3'
Endive	Optional	6 to 8	Late summer for fall harvest	65° - 75°	14 - 21	¼'' deep, 1'' apart	8-12''
Lettuce	Optional	8 to 10	Anytime except midsummer	55° - 65°	14 - 21	½'' deep, ½'' apart	Hd.Rm.12'' Lf.&B thd.8''
Melons: Cantaloupes & Watermelons	Optional	4 to 6	Early summer — after danger of frost	70° - 80°	14 - 21	1'' deep, 4'' apart	Grps.60'' Grps.8-10'
Mustard Greens	No	—	Anytime except midsummer	60° -75°	7 - 14	½'' deep, 5-6'' apart	12''
Okra	Optional	4 to 6	Early summer	70° - 80°	14 - 21	1'' deep, 12'' apart	12-18''
Onions	Optional	6 to 8	Bermuda & Green—late summer Other—early spg. thru midsum.	60° - 75°	14 - 21	¼'' deep, ½'' apart	4''
Parsley	Optional	8 to 10	Late spring through late summer	65° - 75°	21 - 28	¼'' deep, ½'' apart	6''
Parsnips	No	—	Early spring through midsummer	60° - 75°	14 - 21	¼'' deep, 1'' apart	4-6''
Peas	No	—	Very early spring and where winters are mild, late summer	60° - 70°	14 - 21	1-2'' deep, 2'' apart	Rows-2''
Peppers	Optional	10 to 12	Early summer for fall crop	70° - 80°	14 - 21	¼'' deep, 1'' apart	12-18''
Pumpkins	No	—	Early summer	70° - 80°	7 - 14	1'' deep, 4'' apart	Grps.6-8'
Radishes	No	—	Anytime except midsummer	65° - 75°	7 - 14	½'' deep, ½'' apart	2''
Spinach	No	—	Very early spring or late summer	60° - 70°	14 - 21	½'' deep, ½'' apart	4''
Spinach, New Zealand	No	—	Late spring through midsummer	65° - 75°	14 - 21	½'' deep, ½'' apart	4''
Squash, Summer	No	—	Early summer through midsummer	70° - 80°	7 - 14	1'' deep, 3'' apart	Groups-60''
Squash, Winter	No	—	Early summer	70° - 80°	7 - 14	1'' deep, 4'' apart	Groups 4-6'
Tomatoes	Optional	8 to 12	Early summer for fall crop	65° - 75°	14 - 21	¼'' deep, 1'' apart	3'
Turnips	No	—	Early spring and late summer	60° - 75°	7 - 14	½'' deep, ½'' apart	6''

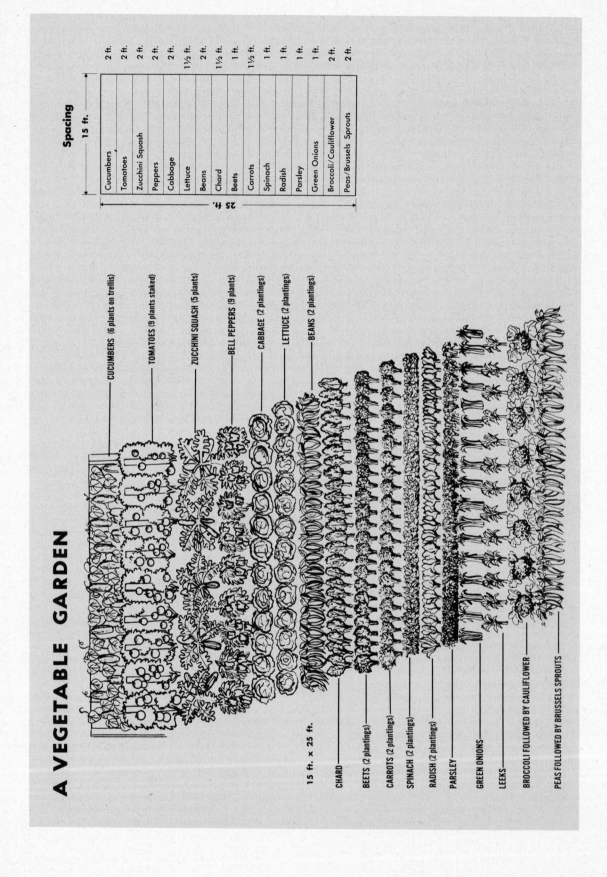

A VEGETABLE GARDEN

15 ft. x 25 ft.

CUCUMBERS (6 plants on trellis)
TOMATOES (9 plants staked)
ZUCCHINI SQUASH (5 plants)
BELL PEPPERS (9 plants)
CABBAGE (2 plantings)
LETTUCE (2 plantings)
BEANS (2 plantings)

CHARD
BEETS (2 plantings)
CARROTS (2 plantings)
SPINACH (2 plantings)
RADISH (2 plantings)
PARSLEY
GREEN ONIONS
LEEKS
BROCCOLI FOLLOWED BY CAULIFLOWER
PEAS FOLLOWED BY BRUSSELS SPROUTS

Spacing

15 ft.

25 ft.

	Spacing
Cucumbers	2 ft.
Tomatoes	2 ft.
Zucchini Squash	2 ft.
Peppers	2 ft.
Cabbage	2 ft.
Lettuce	1½ ft.
Beans	2 ft.
Chard	1½ ft.
Beets	1 ft.
Carrots	1½ ft.
Spinach	1 ft.
Radish	1 ft.
Parsley	1 ft.
Green Onions	1 ft.
Broccoli/Cauliflower	2 ft.
Peas/Brussels Sprouts	2 ft.

Shrubs and vines that grow in the city

American elder
Amur river maple
andromeda
bayberry
bittersweet
Boston ivy
buckthorn
crabapple
English ivy
euonymus
forsythia
honeysuckle
hydrangea
Japanese barberry
red chokecherry
red osier dogwood
scarlet firethorn
Siberian dogwood
spirea
Virginia creeper
witch hazel

Shrubs that grow in dry soils

Amur river maple
bayberry
buckthorn
cinquefoil
common juniper
creeping juniper
evergreen euonymus
myrtle
oleander
privet
red cedar
rosemary
russet buffaloberry
Spanish broom
sumac
tamarix

Shrubs that grow in wet soils

alders
American arborvitae
bayberry
blueberry
Canada yew
dogwood
heather
mountain laurel
red osier dogwood
rosemary
serviceberry

Shrubs that give shade

alder
andromeda
camellia
chokecherry
cypress
dogwood
firethorn
holly
honeysuckle
laurel
leucothoe
mountain maple
periwinkle
photinia
privet
serviceberry
witch hazel

Shrubs that grow in acid soils

arbutus
blueberry
bog rosemary
broom
clethra
common juniper
heath
heather
holly
laurel
leucothoe
rhododendron
serviceberry

Trees for small properties

Amur river maple
broadleaf euonymus
Canada hemlock
English holly
hawthorn
hedge maple
Japanese rnaple
Japanese tree lilac
locust (hybrid honey)
mountain ash
paper birch
Russian olive